I WANT A BOY

I WANT A BOY

Dr Aruna Kalra

Published by
Renu Kaul Verma
Vitasta Publishing Pvt Ltd
4348/4C, Ansari Road, Daryaganj
New Delhi - 110 002
info@vitastapublishing.com

ISBN: 978-81-19670-82-6
© Dr Aruna Kalra
First Edition 2024
MRP ₹450

All Rights Reserved.
No part of this publication may be reproduced, stored in a retrieval system, or transmitted in any form, or by any means–electronic, mechanical, photocopying, recording or otherwise–without the prior permission of the publisher.
The views and opinions expressed in this book are the author's own. The publisher is in no way responsible for the same.

Editorial Team: Tanya Jain, Reena Singh, Saumya & Abhishek Rana
Typeset and Cover Design by Somesh Kumar Mishra
Printed by Chaman Enterprises, New Delhi

Contents

Prologue	*vii*
The Birth of the Goddess	1
Undifferentiated Pain	6
Doctor is a Woman too!	8
Preparation Time	14
Medical College	23
MBBS Final	42
Field Posting and Practical Experience	53
A Doctor at Last!	61
Marriage and My Little Angel	63
Postgraduation and a Labour Case that Haunts till Today	73
Gestational Diabetes Mellitus	81
The Day I Forgot to Scrub	83
MCD Hospital	88
'I want a Boy...' Aarifa's Story	125
My Abortion	130

The Guilt Never Goes…	141
A New Beginning	150
Death is Always Tragic	153
Ray of Hope	166
Doctor can Give You Life	170
A Witness to Complicated Marital Relationships	179
Thrown Out by Second Husband	187
Abortion and Summons	192
Model's Hysterectomy	199
Ayesha's Shattered Dream	207
Fate Always Has Other Plans	211
Sushmita and Shrija	214
A Gynaecologist is Every Girl's Best Friend	220
Obstructed Labour	223
Funny Incidents	229
Infertility (Male Factor)	238
Post-Delivery Blues	242
Father-in-Law as a Sperm Donor	247
My Bhasmasur Act During Covid	253
Twisted Tale: A Funny Covid Story	263
Epilogue	*267*
Acknowledgements	*273*

Prologue

God is with me—he always is. He detached me from everything I was anchored to, so that I could now finish 'this' task. He wants these stories to be out in the light. It took me more than a month to realise that this was really happening—I must enjoy this time, that it would pass if I didn't honour it. Time has stopped for me to tell my story, to fill in those gaps I left out when I was running. I was part of a race that didn't allow me to pause. Thirty years passed in between, and I am still running on a different course, doing different laps, but still racing. Time is racing with me; we are both trying to win. However, I turned out to be a much stronger contestant.

As it rains, I feel the cool breeze on my skin.
I fill my cup with hot tea, my mind with those memories.
I walk again on those forgotten lanes.
I indulge once again in that pain, the sadness,
The helplessness of those forgotten times,
So full of emotion, so full of constant racing.

I didn't dare speak up because I was afraid of lagging behind…

The Birth of the Goddess

(Labour room)

'WHAT IS it, Doctor? Is it a boy or girl? Doctor, please tell me!'

'Will you please shut your mouth for a minute? The doctor is resuscitating your baby!' the nurse replied angrily.

'But you can at least tell whether it's a girl or a boy!'

I didn't want to answer her. 'Let me first stitch your perineum, it's bleeding. The paediatrician is taking care of your baby, he will tell you soon.'

But Sarita knew the answer. It must be a baby girl, that's why no one was answering.

'Tell me doctor, is it a baby girl?'

By the time I had finished suturing, her uterus was very well contracted. Now I could tell her. Many a time I had seen in my practice that the new mother would start bleeding profusely as soon as she got the news that she had delivered a baby girl.

'Sarita, you have given birth to Goddess Laxmi—the goddess of wealth. Who doesn't want Laxmi?' I asked tenderly and touched her head softly.

She started sobbing uncontrollably. The nurses, *aayas*, sweepers and everyone around her began sympathising with her. This was her third girl child.

'Okay doctor, the baby is all right; breastfeeding can begin as soon as possible. Please explain the immunisation schedule to the attendants,' the paediatrician instructed and left to attend another call.

I noticed the mother, still crying, not willing to look at her newborn baby. Meanwhile, the nurses and *aayas* were busy cleaning the instruments, floor, labour bed, preparing it for the next delivery.

'Can't your attendant bring some clothes for you and your baby?' the *aaya* shouted. 'You have been admitted since yesterday; does nobody in your family have the time to bring clothes? Your gown is soiled with blood and urine, how can I shift you?'

'Doctor, there are no clothes for the baby and it's getting cold. What kind of irresponsible people they are!'

I felt sick and nauseous as I watched the scene. This was not my first experience of delivering a girl child. I had seen countless young women weep over having another girl. Which baby would want to come into the world unwanted? Therefore, I prayed for the women who carried them. Every day, I prayed, 'Please God, no girl child again.' But God didn't listen to me; perhaps he had a greater design behind what he bestowed us with.

Like a machine, I was writing delivery notes, but my mind kept wandering somewhere else, restlessly. Sunita Amma, the old *aaya* wrapped the baby in a sterile OT sheet and made her wear an OT scrub gown. This was almost a routine in

government hospitals: disappearing attendants, no changing clothes for the delivering mother or the newborn, no food, tea or coffee for the mother after the exhausting hours of labour.

The *aaya* said to me, 'Doctor, I will not give her the OT gown or sheet, as all of them have made it a habit to take these clothes home. The last time the superintendent made me pay for lost OT sheets. Let them be in soiled clothes! If they are this poor, why don't they deliver at home, why come to the hospital? In our times, we had all our deliveries at home. My sister did all my deliveries, she was a birth attendant at a government hospital, once upon a time. These people can't even pay ₹500 to the home attendant, and look at their audacity, they expect luxury treatment from the hospital. All my five children were born at home. They all are healthy, married now and having kids of their own. In her case, I am not even expecting any tip either! *Mari ne ladki jan di is bar bhi!*'

Aaya was muttering meaninglessly, and I was in no mood to listen to her. 'Please stop it, Amma!' I requested, 'What do you want? You want to leave her in soiled clothes, let her shiver and get sick? For god's sake, cover her with a blanket and wrap the baby in her shawl.'

By now, I assumed that the paediatrician attending the baby or the *aaya* on duty must have informed the relatives about the time of birth and the gender of the baby. I stepped out of the labour room after finishing my notes, called for her people, expecting a cold response as usual. The mother-in-law looked in my direction. She had been speaking with a bunch of women in the waiting area, and all of them had gloomy expressions on their faces.

'God save my son!' she said, in disgust. 'She is a curse on

him, delivering one girl child after the other. My poor son's life is ruined; how will he bear the responsibility of all these girls? My doors to heaven are closed, and without a grandson, my afterlife is ruined too. She will destroy our generation, our genetic lineage.'

All the family members were grieving in unison, worried about the end of their genetic inheritance—the impending doom. Suddenly, the fattest among them and the fairest, came up with a brilliant, successful idea.

'Don't you worry, please convince your son to remarry. I know a beautiful young girl. She's about fifteen years younger than your son, but don't worry, they are poor and without any resources. They will be happy to have your son as their son-in-law, a government servant with a permanent pensionable job.'

With a sparkle in her eyes, she added: 'I will convince them. Don't worry. With God's grace you will celebrate your grandson's birth next year; have faith in the Almighty.'

They ignored my presence, and went on with their insensitive, inhuman blabbering, as if they were dying to make me feel guilty for delivering a baby girl. I wanted to instil some sense into them, to make them understand that it was not the mother's fault or choice. A bunch of females, who had themselves been through the excruciating experience of labour at some point in their lives were abusing, cursing, and spewing venom at another woman, withholding support when she needed it the most.

Realising nobody was coming forward to help the patient, I paid for her tea and biscuits, and requested the nurse to feed the baby with lactose formula, left by one of the previous patients. After an hour, my shift was about to get over and

there was a lot of work which had to be done before that. I gulped my cold tea, and quickly began wrapping up the remaining rounds.

Undifferentiated Pain

ON MY remaining rounds, I witnessed another scene.

'What has happened here, sister? Why didn't you call me?'

'Don't worry doctor, it was her seventh delivery! The baby is all right, she pushed in one go. We couldn't even shift her onto the labour table!' the nurse replied.

'It's okay, let's start intravenous drip and medicine to contract her uterus. She may lose blood from post-delivery bleeding, owing to her grand multi-para status.'

I looked at her stretched uterus, which was feeble in strength. This was bound to happen to patients who had been bearing children like machines. Not only her uterus, but her perineal muscles were weary and gone. Also, her pelvic bones were brittle and barely holding the lady up on her feet.

'What's your name?' I asked.

'Premi Devi,' she replied.

'Look at yourself, you are so pale, no blood in your body. You are looking aged because of repeated deliveries year after year. Why don't you people understand? Why aren't two kids enough for you?'

At this moment, I noticed a few children huddled in a corner of the room.

'Sister, why are these kids here? Who allowed them, how could they pass the gate? Is there no guard?' I shouted.

'Doctor *sahib*, please don't send them out, these are my kids!' I heard a high-pitched voice emerging from the frail, bony woman lying in front of me.

'Doctor, there is nobody out there to attend to them,' the nurse replied.

'No, they can't stay in the labour room, witnessing half-naked ladies, shouting, delivering babies like this.' I protested and asked, 'Where is their father?'

'He is at the traffic light.'

'What do you mean at the traffic light? Why is he or someone not here to look after them?' I asked.

'I mean, he is begging at the traffic light. We migrated from Bihar for work. But only on some days we get labour work, and many months in between we mostly manage without work. We beg at night and try to do small jobs during the day.'

I was aghast!

'And you delivered your seventh child? Why? Why do you want so many children, when you are already in tatters, with no food, no shelter?'

'Doctor, I wanted a son!' the foolish lady muttered.

'I will try again, Doctor! In our village, a son is a must. Moreover, we won't be granted entry to heaven until our sons light our pyres.'

I was stuck, thinking about their deplorable condition, but the clock was ticking.

Rounds, notes, orders.... I needed to be quick.

Doctor is a Woman too!

ONE AFTER the other, I went on revising notes on every bedside. Three of them required immediate Caesarean delivery—they had been in labour for more than thirty hours; one was even leaking. There was arrest in labour. I ordered the nurse to prepare them for OT. The last-minute consent, pre-operative medicines, preloading intravenous were needed before spinal anaesthesia and other procedures.

I was aware that the front room was filling up with new labouring patients every minute. I remembered an old saying which states that almost every second a child is born on this earth.

It's here in India, I guessed that on an average, 50 to 60 children are born per minute. We have many hospitals in our country, and yet every hospital is overfull, brimming with continuous flow of patients. They are multiplying and swarming every single day.

I started examining new labouring patients with lightning speed. I didn't want to leave any pending work for the doctors on night duty.

'Hey Dr Anu, it's five o'clock! Leave it, get going,' the

night shift doctors chuckled.

I raised my head, realising it was dawn already. I fetched my bag and left for the day, only to return to this factory again the next morning.

I entered my car and sat in the driver's seat, turning on the ignition and started for home, exhausted. The car started guiding me, steering itself onto the familiar route. It was like a reflex reaction. My mind was numb, and in no condition to comprehend my surroundings. I paused mechanically at the traffic light, starting again, meandering through the old Delhi roads, crossing Gurgaon, the farm fields, and villages, finally stopping in front of my house.

Throughout the ride back home, I'd kept wondering whether Sarita and her daughter had been taken care of, whether Prema Devi could keep her children with her in the ward or was asked to leave with her newborn.

A few beggar kids appeared on the way, and I noticed they were laughing, and playing happily with each other. Little did they know that every child had a right to proper food, basic education, and good health.

I could hear my daughter crying as soon as I stepped in. It was tough for my mother-in-law to handle my little baby. I rushed in and cradled her in my arms. She seemed to sense my presence, my smell, and smiled.

'She doesn't like the cradle!' My mother-in-law shouted, 'How can I carry her all day? Don't you think I have work? You have spoilt her, carrying her whenever you are at home. Before you go to your room, cook dinner for your father-in-law. He is back from work. Once you are gone with her, she might not allow you to come downstairs.'

I couldn't say anything. I stood dumbfounded in shock, with my daughter in my arms. I had just delivered my baby girl a couple of months earlier and had returned quickly to work to finish my internship at the hospital. I now placed my daughter into the cradle, even though she hated it. With my heart palpitating helplessly, I quickly finished my job in the kitchen, carried her upstairs, pacified her, and breastfed her.

She seemed to transmit her thoughts through each suckle, as if to tell me, 'Mom, I waited for this gentle touch, this tender care, this genuine concern for my discomfort, for my hunger. Where were you? Why did you leave me alone with them? They don't like me. They are simply not interested in my existence. They wanted a grandson, and not me.'

Yes, I still remember their expression of shock and disbelief washing away the joy of them becoming grandparents, as soon as they heard it was a girl.

'No, it can't be true!' my father-in-law said.

He demanded to check the gender of the baby himself. He reacted as if the paediatrician, nurse, and the obstetrician all were playing a dirty trick on him.

'Hand the baby over to me,' my mother-in-law demanded. She seemed to pass the final word, answering the big question: Boy or girl.

The news of the birth of my baby girl was confirmed with their mournful silence. My parents were in the most awkward position, puzzled, wondering whether to offer the sweets on the occasion of their eldest daughter's first born or to stand in the corner with neutral expressions.

My mother-in-law broke the silence, 'It's ok now. Please bring the honey somebody, for the baby's first ritual.'

'But honey is harmful for the newborn. The baby can choke on it. Just breast milk for six months, please!' I protested.

'Don't teach your medicine to me; I have delivered four children. Do you think I killed my babies?' my mother-in-law challenged me.

I looked at my father for support. His cool gaze silenced me.

'Dear, let's not argue with them. We are in no position to contradict. Let's stay quiet and bear this caustic tone silently.'

My father, a senior audit officer in a government job, respected for his immense skills, experience and insight, told me to bear all of this. My father, who had the answer to every question, solution to every problem, for whom the word 'impossible' didn't have any existence, stood in a corner without saying a word. I couldn't bear it or believe it.

My paediatrician husband was also in no mood to discuss the science around the baby's gender, forget about favouring me. So, it was me all alone, defending my point of view, protecting my daughter from these age-old, disastrous myths, like giving honey to a newborn, putting kohl in her eyes, applying oil to every orifice.

For the first time in my twenty-one years of life, I prayed to God. I had never felt the need or the urgency to do it before. Life was beautiful, and full of love and care. My father never let us feel that we were three daughters. Growing up in our family, we had only one stress—of studies.

My father remained unaffected by events around him—whether a financial crisis or office politics. He never complained about the regular visits of relatives to our home or their constant demand that he have a son. He was ever jovial, carefree, and full of life. We were living in his perfect world, where everything was fair, nothing was impossible. It was a picture-perfect world painted with rainbow colours. My father was our protector, guarding us from worldly evils.

But today his armour was pierced. After my marriage, my new family was supposed to play the role of protecting me; instead, they belittled me, manipulated me into thinking it was wrong to bear a daughter. My throat felt constricted with grief. It was too much to take.

When the rituals for the baby started, I directed my gaze towards my daughter, who was fighting with her mouth shut, not letting the honey go in. Seeing the resilience of my newborn, my face relaxed into a smile.

Bravo! My child, you are born as a self-sufficient one, protecting yourself from day one.

She must have sensed the adverse environment, I thought to myself as I saw her struggle. Like all creatures on this earth, transformation, modification, and adaptation are integral parts of survival for homo sapiens as well. This was new to me; seeing a part of my flesh guarding herself independently made me feel proud.

Just after her birth, I had rejoined work. My mother-in-law never forgave me, for she believed I should have taken time off from work to look after my baby till she was at least six months old. But how could I give up my work? I had just finished my MBBS and was still completing my internship, an essential step before a freshly qualified MBBS can apply for postgraduation.

As a doctor, I needed to practice—to be updated with recent advancements, with the newer surgical skills. It was not wise to have spent so many years studying and not pursuing it

further. My individuality, my identity mattered to me; in fact that was the chief purpose of my life.

Ignoring her disapproval, I drove myself to the hospital, meandering through the same roads, spending time with my own thoughts. Five years of MBBS, an year of internship, followed by three years of post-graduation adds up to a total of approximately nine to ten years of studying.

We start at the age of seventeen or eighteen, dedicating tender youthful years of our life to rigorous studies and insane hours of duties in service of patients. By the time we realise that our youth has gone, we still don't feel confident as doctors. Now we require practice to apply our clinical and surgical skills. We need to polish our bookish knowledge and smoothen our surgical techniques. For all of that, a residency for few years is mandatory, preferably in a government hospital with loads of patients. To become a complete and functional doctor, this training was necessary.

The post-delivery months are blue. With a baby in your arms, latched on to your breasts, you are always in physical and mental pain—lack of sleep, backache, pain of stitches, pain in nipples, engorged breasts, constipation, monotony of constant feeding and cleaning poop turns you into a zombie.

One is keen to move on to the next phase. You want to recognise your previous self—an individual who was an enthusiastic bubbly girl with dreams and aspirations. Motherhood is a wonderful feeling. To be a happy and confident Mom, you need to put yourself first. In my case, I was a doctor and I needed to practise being a better doctor, together with the roles one plays in life, first of a daughter, then a wife, followed by motherhood.

Preparation Time

I OFTEN think wistfully of the bygone days when we had filled many premedical entrance forms, CPMT, JIPMER, Wardha, Rohtak, AIIMS, BHU, AMU, AIPMT and CMC Vellore. The fees to the entrance exams were pricey. My duty was to study for the exams and that was all. Filling the forms, identity card, signing it, sending the draft, checking my pencil box for pens and everything else was my father's duty. I still remember the long exam hours, with a break in between.

Many memories crowded my mind—finding the area, the centre (a school) where the exam was to be held, finding the classroom where my roll number was listed, thousands of parents and young kids aspiring to clear the entrance swarming the area near the school, parents waiting patiently for their children to come out after two hours of answering an exhaustive questionnaire. They sat in the shade, on the pavements, the roads, and in nearby shops in the midst of the sultry summer heat.

I remember how my parents rode on a second-hand Lambretta scooter with me. The second-hand scooter was

useful many a times but was painfully heavy to pull especially when it would break down. Sometimes, it could stop in the middle of the journey. A second-hand scooter was a necessity, as my father was finding it difficult to take us everywhere on his bicycle. We were getting heavier, and the distances to our destinations were out of reach. Local transport was also not dependable, so we opted for a faster vehicle. Lambretta was cheaper than Vespa. It didn't last long, but served us well most of the time.

We were upset with my father's choice, and it was embarrassing to stand in the middle of the road often cleaning its spark plug. But my father was proud of his possession. He would patiently clean it, start it every time, and then proceed to explain that every machine had a life, and we shouldn't push it too hard, or get upset with it.

We went to multiple centres to give numerous exams, but the aspiration was simple–to pass with flying colours to become a doctor. I have distinct memories of those exams, how I hated appearing in many of them, but still ended up finishing them, as my father was insistent.

As tired and exhausted as we were, preparing side by side for the twelfth boards and the entrance exams, our faculty and our parents together made us slog for days and months during that excruciatingly hot summer, to bring out the best in us. During revision, we kept reviewing our question paper, counting wrong answers, calculating negative markings and finally analysing our chances of selection.

Physics, chemistry, biology became our nightmares and we also had bad dreams about not finishing our papers in time. In those dry, hot, and dusty summers of May, burdened with frequent power cuts, with no fan or cooler, the exam preparations were literally killing me. I tried sitting in the corridor for some ventilation which I knew was good, but this gave me no relief. Even the water from overhead tanks was too hot for our regular baths, and there was no escape.

It was difficult for my father to manage additional expense for my coaching classes. The monthly fee of ₹500 was a cause of great stress to my parents. I still remember the day I had to join the centre; it was the day my uncle passed away due to cardiac arrest. My parents were away at his funeral. This was during the days long before mobile phones had made an appearance. We couldn't contact each other. I was worried as the fee was to be deposited on the same day, and my parents weren't there. I was stressed, trying to figure out how to go about it. I didn't know what to do.

My father's elder brother was our only relative in the city. But there was no question of requesting the fees from him. He was at the funeral too, and his financial status was the same as ours. Finally, I remembered I could ask for help from our neighbour, my father's best friend, Arora Uncle.

Arora Uncle worked in the electricity department and had a government job. He was rich, affluent, with a well-furnished house and a manicured garden. He and his family respected my simple, humble parents a lot. Though Arora Uncle and his family never liked our neighbours, for they considered themselves higher in status, they somehow liked our family, and were especially fond of my father.

So, when I thought whom to approach for money, the only solution was him. I was hesitant. It was a big amount. I had never seen ₹500-note before. Asking an outrageous amount

of money without my parents' knowledge, was difficult. What if they would feel perplexed and what if my parents could not pay it back? What if Arora Uncle refused blatantly?

But I needed to decide fast. Not much time was left for the class. I was desperate, I needed to do something. If I was not joining with my friends, then I would be in a different batch. I knew I wouldn't be able to study solo. I needed to join now; I couldn't lose this opportunity. On the way to the coaching centre, my mind was calculating the debt—how will we ever be able to pay, how will my father manage next month's fee? How to tell him that I borrowed without his consent? But when I reached the coaching centre that day, the bustling crowd filled me with hope. All of us were set to achieve one goal—MBBS. In my enthusiasm, I forgot about the burden over my head and joined the crowd enthusiastically.

All of us flunked the entrance exams. We didn't get selected even in a single college, based on the dozen exams we appeared for. I took another whole year to prepare for the exams. A lot of my friends joined college and their life began, but mine felt like it was at a standstill.

We lived in a small house. We shared one room amongst us three sisters and our grandmother. There was a double bed for the three of us and a small bed opposite for Dadi. She was a frail, old woman, not fond of girls. The night studies disturbed her, and she would mumble, 'These girls disturb me throughout the night. They are awake the whole night, chatting, giggling, with lights on. I can't sleep in the same room. Let me go to my elder son's house or shift my bed into the kitchen.'

My father was very patient. He knew his elder brother

had a big family of six children and a strict wife. My Dadi too knew she was not welcome in their house. She wanted to stay with them because her grandson was born there. But after a couple of days, their apathy towards her made her return to my parents and to her room with us three, noisy girls. At least we girls were respectful, and both her son and daughter-in-law were dutiful and caring. She lived like a queen with us, always having her way. She was consulted for issues of her interest, mealtimes were fixed, her food was prepared as per her instructions, separate from others, teatime, bath time—everything by the clock. My mom was on her toes all the time, preparing tea, breakfast, cleaning the kitchen, mopping the whole house and the veranda, washing, and sewing clothes, knitting, preparing lunch, dinner, washing utensils at least four times a day, ironing clothes, and in between, cooking fresh meals for Dadi, tea for her friends and so on. She did it peacefully, happily.

Being a mother of three daughters, she didn't have any right to say anything. Besides, she was also very calm, content and a god-fearing lady with no demands, no desires. My Dadi was sarcastic to her in my father's absence. But my mother never complained about her mother-in-law to him. She balanced it well, she understood her, fulfilled her everyday needs quietly, with loving kindness. My Dadi being an orthodox woman, couldn't come to terms with the fact that my mother couldn't bear any son. However, in her heart of hearts, silently, she was fond of my mother.

I remember my mother buying thin *mulmul* (muslin) salwar kameez for my Dadi in summers to beat the heat and for the winters, she knitted woollen kneecaps, leg covers and

scarves for her as my Dadi was frail and couldn't bear either hot summers or harsh winters. She didn't like our gender, but I believe she loved us and cared for us. My mom told me that during my toddler days, my grandma massaged me with pure ghee, and fed me full cream milk. She loved us, but she loved her grandson more as he was supposed to be the heir of the family. In that one room, we grew up together, we three girls along with our Dadi.

Meanwhile, I dreamed about becoming a doctor. I thought about all those times I used to play 'doll' games with my sisters and neighbouring girls. All five of us had handwoven dolls—my Mom had sewn three, one for each of us.

My doll, with her square face, square body, thin arms, and legs, ugly looking with long, black woollen hair, was a doctor. Her hair was just like mine, long, thick, falling till the hips and she had a white apron made to order by mom. I wondered whether being a doctor was a passion or obsession rooted in my inner being since then! When we played this game on our terrace, I made sure no other doll was allowed to become a doctor. We fought tooth and nail on this every other day. I played alone with my doll in desperate times but would allow no compromise on my dream. But my dream was shattered when I failed. I wasn't meritorious enough to get a seat out of 30,000!

This was a phase when I doubted my ability to sustain my studies and mental strength for the following year. Also, I was doubtful of my father's ability to sustain the expensive tuition fee every month. When I got admitted to the special coaching centre run by that dark, fat, bald teacher of biology, infamous for being a drunkard, little did I know what destiny had in store for me. All I remember was the hectic and crazy traffic of the marketplace where the coaching centre was, travelling the nine kilometre-stretch by cycle, the rich, elite students studying there, the distracting sound of the Bharatnatyam classes just above the centre, and my mental association with it, as dance was my second passion, apart from my desire to be a doctor. I also remember the obsession of people watching B R Chopra's epic series *Mahabharata* on Sundays when we paddled along the almost empty roads to reach the centre.

My goal was clear, to get admission in medical college. All other things could follow after that. After our crash coaching for three months, we had hopes that maybe a few of us could crack the exams.

I remember the pain my father went through every time he checked my role number in newspapers and was disappointed. I didn't clear a single premedical test. I remember my mom telling me that I was born in Lady Harding Hospital in Delhi. She told us she wished to see me as a doctor in that hospital one day.

She thought it would be an easy commute from Ghaziabad. But there was only one bus from ALT Centre in Ghaziabad to Shivaji Stadium opposite Lady Harding Medical College. Shivaji Stadium Bus Stop was called Madras Hotel in the old days, after the name of the famous cafe in Connaught Place. How simple was her logic and her desire. But how distant was this dream, and so unachievable.

I still remember that eventful day when a postal slip arrived at our address. God was with me.

I had got selected! A thin brown strip of paper was thrown into my veranda by the postmaster on a bicycle. It flew under my charpoy as a strong wind blew. I caught it just before it was

blown out on the road to be lost in the trash, forever. Imagine, my fate was written on that paper strip and it depended fully on our postal system. I was fortunate that it was delivered and that I managed to retrieve it just on time.

'You are selected, please come to meet the dean in Lucknow,' it read.

Difficult to comprehend at first, I tried to grasp its meaning and wondered how to react. Was it true? I was being called to join a medical college!

I showed it to my father. With high hopes and optimism, we packed our clothes, and boarded a train to Lucknow. After an overnight journey, we stayed in a retiring room on the platform, and then headed towards the dean's office in the medical college. The peon asked us to wait for a while. A few more students were sitting with their parents awaiting their turn.

The college was old, with a high ceiling, built in a Victorian style with burnt red bricks, widespread lawn with ancient trees as witness to its history. The ancient trees stood solemnly, with depth and composure, providing cool wind and green shade. We could see doctors in aprons, teachers, nurses, gardeners and many more office people going about their business around the official building. We also noticed the clean, cemented floors, the walls painted in two colours, beige and dark brown.

We were sitting quietly, holding my certificates, mark sheet, and that postal slip in a zipped bag. Eventually, the peon called us inside the huge room, and the dean was sitting on the other side of an old wooden table, a very gentle, elderly man, dressed humbly, a few strands of hair sticking to his scalp. He requested us to be seated.

We greeted him and my father introduced himself before making himself comfortable on the chair. We presented that piece of paper and wanted him to crack the code for us. Did this slip meant what we understood? Had I secured a seat?

Instantly, he disclosed the most awaited news of my life.

'Yes, you got the seat in medical college. You were in the waiting list; what would you like to join, MBBS or BDS,' the dean asked.

It was unbelievable, I was in a dream! Just like that God had granted my wish in an instant. Then he offered his advice.

According to him, BDS was preferable for girls, as postgraduation in it was not mandatory. I had an option to choose any—BDS from King George Medical College, Lucknow, or MBBS from B R D Medical College, Gorakhpur. In his opinion, KGMC was far reputed in terms of merit and asked me to choose it. Nonetheless, he gave me a few minutes to discuss with my father before picking my seat.

My father was influenced by the dean's genuine, honest advice, but I wanted to become a doctor, not a dentist. I was determined. There were no second thoughts and I chose the MBBS seat in Gorakhpur. That day paved the way to my future.

What if I was not in the veranda that day and hadn't noticed that postal slip? What if my father was on a tour for a few days? What if the postal service had not delivered the letter? My destiny would not have been the same then.

All my friends, by then, were in college. Some had joined vocational courses—stitching, cooking course, computer typing, data analysis, while others had opened boutiques or worked in marketing. If circumstances were different, this could have been my fate as well.

Medical College

AS FRESHERS, we were to share our rooms—two girls in one room. During the first two years, it was mandatory to share a room with another girl, your peer, as no one would get a single room. The process of getting the room was a great gamble. If by sheer luck, the peer sharing your room, happened to be a hardworking, diligent, meritorious student having the same temperament as yourself, your life would be easy, otherwise you would be stuck in a bad environment, and that was a common phenomenon. But whatever the conflicts, you and your roommate were supposed to put aside all your differences and arguments and were expected to resolve all issues within the confines of your room. In case it went out of the room, you would be judged or worse, stigmatised.

My roommate was a proud girl, rich, charming, a dusky beauty with thick long black hair, curly eyelashes, and an hourglass figure. Despite her arrogance and fiery temperament, I didn't fail to notice her charisma. At the very outset, she decided that I was not fit to be her roommate. She tried to push me to another girl's room, but I was too naive and frightened to change the room given to me. I thought it was like an arranged marriage—unchangeable and invincible. I was convinced that if one could not compromise to make a relationship better, things would be the same in every relationship in life.

Our relations turned sour because of our completely different ways of living. Her waking and sleeping hours were very different than mine, her habits of not bathing daily and not washing her underclothes felt filthy. Our room was messy all the time, with dirty utensils piled up in one corner for days together, until I would clean them! Though she would use my utensils as well, cleaning them was always my job. She was used to having maids at home and was a spoilt brat. It seemed quite normal for her not to share simple everyday responsibilities. She would never even clean the room or the bathroom, and her dirty clothes were always piled in there. On the other hand, her extravagant ways of life irked me immensely. She would party every other day in our room, inviting other fashionable girls and seniors, fooling around, and merrymaking. At other times, she would be studying secretly in their room. Her indifferent ways, her ruthless, unkind behaviour, left me feeling uncomfortable and lonely every single day.

Each one of my peers had become good friends with their roommates. Many of the girls made friends with their citymates too. There were groups like the Ghaziabad girls, Moradabad girls etc. But I was sidelined even by those groups. My companions on the train, with whom I had journeyed from Ghaziabad to Gorakhpur, were also not interested in me. They hung around together all the time, all the Ghaziabad

girls—whether they went to the canteen, to attend classes in college, or to hang around in the library. Back in the hostel, they sat in one of their friend's rooms for hours together chatting, gossiping, laughing till midnight.

As for myself, I was always a loner, never taking part in any of this; it troubled me a lot. At that very tender age, I craved to be a part of a group or team, like everybody else. I craved for validation, for acceptance among peers. In my heart of hearts, I craved to be heard, to participate in silly, trifling things which everyone else did. I had left behind a nice group of school friends, and I missed their company. I would sit alone and friendless in my room every day. Moreover, medical studies were overwhelming and the pressure on me was enormous.

Anatomy was the first subject in our medical studies and reading it from the book by Chaurasia made it difficult and nightmarish for us students. I wondered how such an interesting subject could be turned into a mockery by colour coding the pages in red, blue, and yellow. One needed to have a photographic memory to memorise the contents of its pages. Every page looked similar, and we all had a really hard time understanding, and cramming its contents, and focusing on repeated revisions of the chapters.

To do it all successfully, we needed study partners.

We needed to make sense of the pictures. We needed to understand and memorise where the muscles of the human body started, how they were wrapped around the bone and how it was inserted to the other end of the bone. We needed to understand the path of vessels and nerves in the human body, how they were traced on the bone, so that we could understand their function. And to remember the lesson better, a study partner was an essential prerequisite, especially for better marks, better viva preparation, and of course, for a confident poster presentation. I was seeing how the girls around me made study partners, studying, dining, sleeping, living every moment of their lives together, in total sync with one another during those five years of their medical studies. If the room partner and study partner happened to be the same, it was like hitting the jackpot.

I could still visualise that petite, fair girl I was back then. I still remembered how soft-spoken and timid I had been, how low my self-confidence was in those days. But surprisingly, despite my meek nature, people around were jealous of me. This truth was conveyed to me at our 25th reunion. Honestly, I wasn't aware of it till then. However, I was feeling the brunt of it without even having a hint. In the lecture hall, I could see senior boys hovering around me and my roommate. Our senior girls teased me about their batchmates; still the ignorant me didn't get any clue.

Our first year in college was really a trying time. We went to college together in a single line, came back in queue, all fifty girls huddled together. In between, everything that I did was pursued alone. I studied alone, sat alone, and I was quiet, maintaining distance from everyone. Looking back at those days of my medical studies, some memories and images stood out distinctly, and the memory of the dissection hall happened to be one among those.

The dissection hall was huge with tall glass windows on both sides from ceiling to floor, opening its view to grounds full of dried long grass and scattered trees. The hall didn't need

electric lights; the rays of the sun lit the room with their bright, natural light. I distinctly remember two rows of dissection tables, decorated with cadavers on both sides of the long hall, like OT tables surrounded by chairs. I also clearly remember the dead bodies placed at each table, stinking of formalin and some stale burnt smell. It felt as if the smell tore through my nostrils to pierce my brain.

Breathing was tough in that hall. If one tried to breathe through the mouth, the throat went dry and itchy. It was nauseating. The dissection period started from noon every day and lasted till evening. A batch of ten was allotted one cadaver, divided into groups of two for each extremity dissection. Our dissection lesson included the head and neck, upper arm, thorax, abdomen, and pelvis, lower limbs, and neuro anatomy. This practical session of dissection was preceded by our reading of both *Cunningham's Manual of Practical Anatomy* and Dr Chaurasia's book of *Human Anatomy*, and I still wonder why we had to read them. They neither helped us during exams nor in life.

Taken away from our familiar world of books with simple English and explanatory paragraphs, the text in Cunningham was scattered in between lengthy, brain-numbing descriptions. We lived in perpetual confusion and bewilderment, as we bought the expensive Cunningham, and couldn't make out how to extract the relevant information. Hence, we studied anatomy all along with B D Chaurasia's anatomy book, which was oversimplified. Its absolute simplification made it equally tough to understand, however easy it was to mug up. The rule was quite simple, we needed to memorise the text to pass the exams and get through the viva. This viva was conducted after each body part's dissection, for example upper arm, head, and neck.

While all this was happening, we also had some interesting moments in class. Around the table with our companion cadaver, we made fun of each other, including the cadaver (we treated him or her like our friend, regardless of their circumstance of death). Though our teachers went mad because this meant showing disrespect to a dead body, we nevertheless felt he or she was also our partner in crime. When we accidentally cut an important nerve or an artery, it was his or her (cadaver's) duty to cover for us. Gradually, with time, we got accustomed to the dissection hall and to those pungent and burning fumes of the 'formalin environment', as we called it.

I still remember my very first day standing beside that cadaver; the smell and sight was intoxicating me. I had almost fallen on the floor. I was taken to the professor's chamber to recover from the vasovagal shock. Surrounded by all the boys in my class, I felt important as people comforted me, offered me water, and fussed over me. However, we all were aware that it was only a pretext to escape the anatomy class. It was an exciting moment, nonetheless.

Another incident which defamed our batch boys and harmed them to a great extent also happened in the dissection hall. A class was going on when it happened. All the students had gathered around the blackboard on their stools. Some were standing behind it due to lack of seats. Dr Shyam ji, professor of anatomy was explaining the lower extremity with much interest, explaining the details of every nerve route, muscle attachment and their action, among other things.

Suddenly, a piece of chalk hit the bald part of his head. A six feet tall man walked in defiantly, as if he owned the college. A former student of this college and a "thug" at heart, he was a man with good academic standing. As a young man he had mesmerised all the girls during his college days.

Back then, he and his friend had fought for a girl, and it soon turned into a love triangle. Shyam ji got stabbed in the tussle and scored high in love. Naturally, the girl who was now his wife, had fallen for him back then as he was ready to die to win her. The other fellow, Dr Tiwari, who happened to be his best friend back then, was also working here as PSM professor. Their relationship was visibly strained now. The victorious Shyam ji walked like a king, looking down at Dr Tiwari and all others, thinking of himself as a superior entity. He was infamous as a tough senior, who advocated a severe form of ragging to keep the young freshers grounded. For the first time, someone had dared to hit him with chalk on his bald head during one of his classes! Few giggled, while others were awestruck, or simply frightened. The incident was unbelievable and unimaginable.

That very moment, the shocked, furious Shyam ji ordered all the girls to leave the dissection hall immediately. All the boys inside the class were now alone with Shyam ji, the thug. In that moment, he was transformed into a senior again, and he kept hitting all the boys asking for the name of the person who had thrown the chalk. Dumbfounded with shock, the boys could hardly speak; they knew the consequences would be dangerous for that fellow. The boys had been playing between themselves when the chalk accidentally hit him, but how could anyone disclose that fact! For almost half an hour, they were shouted at and hit and there was much noise and crying. Senior boys from the hostel and from the hospital ran to help Shyam ji and to teach the boys of our batch a good lesson for their outrageous, unpardonable offence.

It was sad to watch the boys bleeding through their noses, limping with their broken bones and disheveled hair. The young boys, toiling away from the comfort zones of their homes were brutally beaten, and were shocked to the core. No senior sympathised with them. Another round of hitting awaited them from their seniors in the hostel. The brutal process of ragging went on for several weeks, but the secret regarding the chalk and who aimed it at Dr Shyam ji was buried forever. Dr Shyam ji wanted to teach us a lesson for posterity so that we would always remember the consequences of any action we did. He sent shivers down our spine and he succeeded in it. No one ever spoke about it ever again, as if the topic seemed cursed to us.

After twenty-five years, when we met during our silver jubilee batch meet, the hidden truth was revealed to all. It was a painful memory with no consolation whatsoever. The secret came out and we walked through that lane in our memories, as fresh as if it had happened just yesterday.

There were numerous rumours and stories which kept floating in the air—to believe or not to believe was the question. The college had become our family for five long years—affairs, fights, and scandals had been part and parcel of our lives during those days. Competition for better scores in stage (study of one body part) completion, poster presentation, preparing for our final exams were our day-to-day realities. Studying secretly, hiding notes, taking help from our seniors, trying to jack up our marks with the help of doctor parents or by seducing professors, all was acceptable.

It was also an open secret that one of our senior batch girls was sleeping with Dr Shyam in his chamber or in his house. She was a very beautiful girl, with long delicate fingers. During dissection, it was a feast to watch her delicate fingers (even in gloves) intricately playing with muscles in search of camouflaged nerves and arteries. He appreciated her soft, long, smooth fingers and her talent in dissection. For him, the pleasure of accomplishing a good dissection was orgasmic, and everyone knew it.

Gupta sir was one of the macho men in the Department of Anatomy. We considered both the two professors as Kapil Dev and Gavaskar. Gupta sir was short, bald, charismatic, intelligent, well-read, quiet and composed. He was a man of a few words, throwing in sarcastic humour here and there whenever he spoke. It was a treat to have a conversation with a man who was so gifted academically and held brain-stimulating views. His romantic face was largely obscured by the six feet tall, chivalrous and more adventurous Shyam ji, but he had his share of fun here and there. A girl from our batch, a Kashmiri beauty revealed excitedly that Gupta sir had shown her a live swimming sperm under the microscope. And everyone in the hostel guessed the source of the live sperms. It was quite clear that he had masturbated in her presence. The hostel air was rife with all these stories and hypotheses.

College strike: One major campaign erupted in our time, causing our entire batch an unwanted delay of six months, compared to other colleges. The crisis started with a sudden loss of electricity in the boys' hostels. Studying proved difficult.

After returning to the hostel, there was no water to freshen up or to take baths, especially after hectic hospital duties.

Having to live without water, and without fans to nap under before reporting for duty, was both painful and frustrating. Sometimes the authorities provided water tanks. All the boys, senior or junior, had to stand in queues to fill their buckets. In that way, they were deprived of the opportunity to be in their classes, in their labs or libraries. The time they should have been spending on research and taking care of patients was instead spent in queuing up for one bucket of water.

All hell broke loose when they revolted after a few days. An agitated crowd raided the dean's house, vandalised it and discovered new air conditioners, fans, water dispenser and other hidden treasures in the back rooms. Evidently, all such equipment had been allocated for the college. The news spread like wildfire and the dean's corruption was exposed. At the college, we all became part of a revolution, a movement of protest until the dean resigned. Thus, instead of studying for our first professional exam that was merely a few months away, we were summoned to go on a strike, to become part of a huge crowd of protestors.

I clearly remember the tent put up in front of the entrance with its raised platform that had been set up for sitting, and for shouting our protest slogans and showcasing the hunger-stricken young doctors. The hunger strike went on for a couple of weeks. It was indeed a chaotic situation. The college was shut, and only emergency services were running in the hospital.

Our hospital catered to patients from Bihar, Nepal border, and remote UP villages. It was a poor belt, with

our college being the only available medical facility, nearby. Those days, the endemic of Japanese Encephalitis had been spreading in and around Bihar, Basti, Gorakhpur and other surrounding towns. Hundreds of children were dying of JE fever, hypoglycaemia and neurological symptoms. Even if the children survived, they would have to live with permanent brain damage. Malnutrition, excessive summer heat with no monsoon rains, scarcity of water and food were the everyday realities, and that worsened their condition, leading them to their deathbeds.

Under such circumstances, the already malnourished kids with no reserve of glucose in their livers, had fallen prey to dehydration of their bodies, resulting in fatal infections. These famished kids of below ten years started developing high grade fever, which dehydrated them further. Starvation led to convulsions and delirium and the doctors had to watch helplessly, as they slipped into coma.

Although this was a memory from 1991, nothing much had changed for these patients till 2020. The hospital still caters to young children, many of them less than 10 years old who seek treatment for some deadly and devastating diseases, some of which are completely preventable. Ironically, we haven't been able to cure hunger in all these thirty years.

But going back to those times again, it was the period of Japanese Encephalitis, and to make matters worse, the hospital had shut its services to the sick and needy. The doctors who were supposed to treat them were on a hunger strike.

We got ready every morning as usual to march in a single line, in our white salwar kameez, black dupatta, and our oiled hair. We believed we had to participate in the revolution to bring about real change. Our days were full of activities. We would sit on the platform, hungry for days till the second group would take over, then make posters, sticking them on the city walls, making banners, placards, postcards, even sending them to the Prime Minister of India, and going to the post office to deliver hundreds of postcards daily. Collecting money from shop owners and from pretty much everyone at traffic lights on footpaths, we begged, we polished shoes, we sold popcorn and fruits to collect money for our cause. We requested sellers on carts, sellers sitting by the roadside and other menial workers to lend their goods to us to sell on the busy main roads of Gorakhpur. Meandering through traffic, bringing it to a halt sometimes, we forced commuters to buy those goods at exorbitantly higher prices as instructed by our seniors.

We needed funds for the uninterrupted running of this strike. And so, with all our enthusiasm, we marched into the city every day, holding banners, placards, requesting people to help us. Sometimes, we sat on pavements and offered to shine the shoes of pedestrians! At other times, we went to bigger corporates for donations. Our college was on the outskirts, some 15-20 kms from the city. It took about half an hour in a paddle rickshaw and fifteen minutes in Vikram autos—a bunch of cheap, shared autos—we had in those days that stopped every few metres to drop and pick up passengers. I remember how we had to sit crammed inside the auto, waiting for it to fill up, then holding tight to prevent ourselves from falling as it gathered speed. I remember the multiple back and forth trips the autos made, to earn the maximum amount for the day—the young drivers racing with the others, overtaking them, abruptly cutting in front of them to fetch a passenger

waiting ahead. The entire scene looked like a live video game race, with the overtaking, speeding, toppling over each other, with no concern for the safety of the passengers, which often included pregnant women.

We travelled through these autos regularly during our protest days to garner sympathy and collect donations for white coat medical students. Finally, the dean buckled and resigned. The hospital and college resumed their regular function. Exams were announced and in just a couple of weeks, we had to finish all the coursework—anatomy, physiology, biochemistry, and embryology. We requested for postponement, but our wish was turned down. We were already lagging behind the other colleges. The next few weeks, everyone studied without a pause. No one wanted to fail and join the junior batch. It was totally unacceptable to all, including the juniors.

But despite all this, college was fun. We celebrated sports and cultural weeks every year, the only time we would abandon our studies. Sports like table tennis, badminton, cricket, basketball, volleyball, carrom, and stage performances such as singing, dancing, plays, and much more filled those days. After morning classes, matches would begin. The girls would gather around to cheer for their batchmates, hooting and egging them on to overpower their opponents. The whole batch participated and gathered for each game, girls match, night cricket, boys' and girls' doubles. The ones who didn't play were active in cheerleading. Others were active in the cultural sphere.

The air was full of excitement and enthusiasm, and everyone kept their spirits high. Winning for the batch was the motto. The sports week was held in winters. We all used to sit around the court, merrily munching peanuts, gossiping, eyeing those smart, senior boys, and wondering why they were not our boyfriends. Such pointless conversations and laughter continued till midnight. As our mindless banter went on, we would notice fresh couples sneaking out to 'love lane', a dark, isolated road with a dead end.

Stage and field practices went on till the wee hours of the morning. My memories of those times consist of rounds of tea, rehearsals, conflicts over dance steps, disagreements over song selection, play dialogues, choice of actors and so on. Often, conflict ensued between our seniors and ourselves over practice time at stage. Seniors being seniors, always pushed our rehearsals to late night hours.

Our senior batch was super talented. Their batch had singers with gifted voices, who could compete with Rafi, Kishore, or Manna Dey. Girls were gifted enough to compete with Lata and Asha Mangeshkar. When they sang, the whole auditorium fell silent. The audience demanded the performers to sing more, after one song ended. I can still recall their soulful, melodious voices in perfect sync with instruments, rhythm, and beats. The presentation, idea and performance of the dancers were excellent too. I was in love with our immediate senior batch. They were rich in every aspect, good looking, humorous, level-headed singers, and dancers, and very much in sync and in unity with each other. They themselves were proud of this fact.

Our batch was bigger, and we were not as gifted in artistry as our seniors, but we were fiercely competitive. We scored first position in field dance and third in stage group dance in our first year. Winning over our seniors felt intoxicating and

gave us a triumphant feeling.

During all this melange of diverse activities, exams and extracurricular programmes, the college became our second family. It was a small world of our own, within the periphery of those premises. Our bond with the teachers and seniors grew over time, and defined our lives back then, even if we were severely ragged by our seniors during our freshman days.

Once it was time for a new batch's arrival, a grand party happened. It would take place in our hostel a night before and in the college the next night. It was a ball.

We were supposed to choose our favourite seniors. These seniors would be our guardians for the rest of our years in medical college. We needed to make small handwritten slogans for them and vice versa. Everyone knew about their choices. The seniors were excited to get their pet juniors, as they would be the ones helping them during their exams, getting food from the mess, and making tea at nights, drawing in manuals, completing their journals etc. In turn, they helped us with our exams and viva, while reciprocating equally in all other areas. I chose my medical moms without calculating future benefits, though all others weighed their choices using their foresight.

I was happy with my medical guardians. However, during the same time, many enemies were also made—enemies who were somehow anticipating my partnership with them. The seniors who were very hospitable and friendly in their attitude with me before, suddenly became aloof and unkind. They stopped coming to my room. I could sense their detachment and started feeling lonely all over again.

A bunch of seniors had thought I had rejected them despite all the love they had showered on me. There was a time during my hostel days when they had supported me immensely, particularly when I was alone without any good roommate. They consoled me when I was crying all day. They believed I would choose them because we shared a common bond. We were either from the same city or their batchmates liked me, so it felt like there was some kinship. Unfortunately, the chemistry had changed with time after that ceremony of senior selection. They began to make fun of me and made my life a bit difficult.

Nonetheless, the ceremony went fine. We exchanged gifts. One-liner slogans were read aloud to praise or tease each other. That night, our seniors seemed compassionate. Dr Asthana, our professor, had organised the next day's ceremonial dinner, the welcome party for freshers, the last day of our white dress march past and liberation.

Next night we had a gala dinner at the college hall. We were supposed to choose our medical spouse for the occasion, just for fun. It was a special night where we, the girls, dolled up in sarees, and boys in tuxedos. All teachers and faculty were invited for the celebrations. I still remember the paper crowns given to us with weird slogans on them. Boys were supposed to wish their medical moms by lying flat on the floor, touching their senior girls' feet. Apparently, this was their last day of ragging. Senior girls hovered around junior boys, ordering them to do bizarre tasks, like eating four sweets in one go or shouting, 'you love me'. It was a fun-filled night, when the division between seniors and juniors got blurred, putting an end to the ragging episodes. Everyone became equal and had a lot of fun. We danced till midnight, intoxicated with the festivities.

Then it was time for Medifest—a medical festival. When

this happens, the whole college gears up for it. All batches from the first year to the final year participate in well-organised sports events: badminton singles and doubles, cricket, basketball, volleyball, 100-meter race, table-tennis, indoor games, carom, etc. They also participate in cultural activities with many verticals: field dance, solo performances, group dances, singing, mimicry, plays, instruments, and much more.

The subjects in the third year were boring, but some of our studious batchmates were always busy memorising everything. On the other hand, I was in my element, practising my solo dance, teaching group dance to girls and boys, till the early hours of the mornings. Practice would go on long after college, and we gathered in the college corridors.

Post 5 pm, college was deserted. But there was another issue at hand: students of all batches showed up, knowing it was empty, trying to grab a place for themselves for practice. The auditorium stage was reserved for the senior batch, and so they wouldn't allow any juniors to practice till they finished.

Once we had the place all to ourselves, we indulged in a *chai* party, practised, debated dance steps and pairings, engaged in petty fights, and celebrated together. But these were the best part of college days. The intensity of our performance preparation felt like we were gearing up for a battle against both seniors and juniors. Those chilly December nights were not so cold. In the heat of hooting, encouraging our classmates on their matches, sitting under shared shawls, and munching on groundnuts, exchanging special glances with potential boyfriends were all part of a beautiful memory. But these things also distracted us. I realised that I hadn't studied a bit and was not aware that the exam would fall on my head like a boulder.

Seniors were convinced that it would be postponed. In my make-believe bubble, I was enjoying my dance practices till late in the night, sleeping in the class the next morning, and because of that, I almost flunked in the third year. Thankfully, I was helped by my batchmate, who was sailing in the same boat as me, and together, we hit the books with all the seriousness we could muster. We studied together to barely finish the course once.

Medifest was like the Olympics for us. Students who were better in extracurricular activities than medical curriculum were shining. Boys and girls who were not very talented were around for behind-the-curtain activities, to keep our spirits high. It was a time of making friends with our batchmates and several of them hitched up together. A few new couples emerged, amongst them a few lasted and got married, and a few slowly drifted apart under the stress of studies.

Many students protested to delay the exams, to get more time for studies; I prayed for the same but didn't want to waste time on meeting teachers, and getting petitions signed by many. I knew I would be glad if exams were postponed, but because I didn't see that happening, I started preparing. I felt like crying the syllabus seemed taller than Everest. It was not possible for me to pass this time. For the first time in the examination hall, the question paper seemed like it had come from some other subject; everything seemed foreign—Greek or Latin. These were the worst exams of my life.

I prayed to God and pleaded, 'Please, save me this year, and I will be studious from the next year. Please don't let me slip down to the junior batch.'

You lose all your friends from your batch if that happens. Juniors never make friends with you as you are a failed senior. You are suspended in a no gravity zone between two batches, belonging to none. This is the worst situation, for one is attending classes alone, eating alone, and is not involved with either batch.

MBBS Final

IT WAS time for the fresher batch to join our college. We were seniors now.

It was a tradition in our medical college that seniors had to protect their juniors even when outside the premises. Seniors were supposed to pay, if they were in the same auto or city bus, or if they happened to be in the same restaurant. Seniors were supposed to escort freshers from the railway station when they arrived to join the college with their parents. According to the roster, four students went to fetch the juniors and their parents from the bus or railway station each day.

In my group, a Kashmiri girl, a boy, and I were together, and incidentally the fourth person didn't turn up. We were strolling on the platform, talking softly. The boy and Kashmiri girl knew each other from their previous college. The boy was smart, witty, and moody. He had a cousin who was a few batches senior. There were clear instructions to the other senior boys to not touch him on the pretext of ragging. He considered himself superior to us, looked down upon his own batchmates, and didn't mingle with any of us. He was seen with senior boys all the time. I thought of him as an arrogant, sporty but charming person. He had his way when we were suffering through the gruelling ragging discipline. That's what I found attractive about him.

He would manage to get good grades in his exams, though he was not exceptionally intelligent. He befriended a Muslim girl in our batch, whose drawing skills were amazing. She could infuse life into her art. We had a poster competition in Physiology and Anatomy, and this girl painted a masterpiece. Her artwork was a cut section of femur (thigh) bone, and each blood vessel was drawn with such intricate detail. We visited her room every day to see the progress on it, till she finished.

She was a fine artist, and a very patient one. One month before the competition, she started working on this poster. Our chance to get the award was bleak, and we knew that very well. She sat for hours together to work on it, slowly, cautiously, with precise flawless movements. She worked on it religiously and the poster was a knockout, a magnificent showpiece. It was going to be put up on the college wall. We were proud of her, the hard work and dedication earned respect from all our batchmates till she revealed that it was to be presented as the work of this clever boy. He had requested her to make a poster for him. She withdrew her participation because quite understandably, she couldn't manage to make two masterpieces. And the poster adorned the wall of the college with the signature of this astute boy.

That day on that railway platform, that clever boy asked me out—an invisible, unpopular girl and a domineering, frisky and fascinating boy. He was attracted to me. Opposites attract!

I was drawn towards him for his clever ways, his ability to get everything done with ease, his ability to manipulate people, and his ability to rule over his own batch boys. During those days, I discovered that I was feeling a pull towards flamboyance. Among our batch of 120 students, he was the only boy I admired, and this proposal had come out of the blue! I couldn't get over it for a very long time. The pause and silence on my part frightened his ego. He quickly gathered his wit, and to avoid any chance of rejection, he offered his friendship till I felt sure about any relationship with him. I rejected that too. I didn't want to and I repented it throughout my MBBS years. He made sure to make me realise that it was a blunder. I liked him, but was never quite sure about our relationship. He could be deceitful to me as well.

During those days, having boyfriends was quite taboo, even though I knew that my father wouldn't have objected. Life would've been so easy with a partner beside you, and I had always envied our seniors who coupled together everywhere. His influential status would have helped me too. However, I still wonder why despite the lure to be in love, I chose to be alone. Perhaps I was just scared.

That day was one of the most memorable days in my life. It felt like my first love, whereas in reality, we never even became friends. When we looked at each other, our eyes spoke in a suggestive, unexplained language. Neither was I clear what to say to him, nor had he the courage to approach me again. There were many hints from him, but I was never sure if those hints were serious. I was not sure whether I was ready for this or if I could deal with it. I wondered what might happen if it turned out to be a joke when I finally had the guts to

reciprocate. It was a big risk, when I was already being bullied for not having a friend. I was called to his parties where people wondered, why me! I wasn't part of their western UP group, after all.

They were among the two most prominent groups. One was the Western UP, English-speaking group, consisting of the well off, prim and proper crowd and another was the Eastern UP group, high on merit but low on social skills, and lacking good dress sense. They didn't speak in English at all. All the boys in the Western UP group were staunch chauvinists. On the other hand, the Eastern UP boys, studying in Hindi medium schools, had never ever spoken to girls in their life.

I was getting hints of small favours from him, directly or indirectly. He was close to the senior boys as well as girls. He was everywhere, in sports and cultural events, in gatherings with very senior PG boys, with faculty members, and even in teachers' parties. He manipulated his way into the system. His batchmates and peers knew his manipulative nature and were somewhat afraid of him because of his connections. It occurred to me soon that it was better to have him as a friend.

Once, he was my partner in a group dance. It was then that he reached out to me, sending me messages through the Western UP girls. I could have slipped if those girls didn't warn me to stay away from him. He sent me his shirt for a Haryanvi dance; we needed to wear an oversized boy's shirt over our lehenga. The messenger girl from the Western UP group delivered it and requested me to stay away from him for my own safety.

I had known then that being associated with him would be detrimental to my life, but his presence, the attention he showered on me was addictive. I loved watching him play table-tennis. Cheerleading for him during volleyball matches was exhilarating, even if his team lost most of the time because of him. Once I lied for him and it felt like a great deal.

In an early morning lecture, where attendance was always poor, two boys from the last row said something abusive about our professor. It was true that the professor was no good in his subject because he kept mumbling, without really explaining anything. The professor turned around angrily. I knew the boys who had passed the remark. It was the one I liked, besides another fellow. His eyes met mine, silently pleading with me to not reveal his name. I was one of the backbenchers that day. The teachers called me to their chambers for a final confirmation. As I was the only one who witnessed it closely, I knew the punishment would mean a year's loss for the student. That student would have to move to the junior batch for the whole of his MBBS course. Did anyone deserve such severe punishment for a bit of teenage fun, I wondered. But the teachers at our college were merciless.

This time it was bad as the future of two boys depended on my statement and identification. It felt bad to lie. I couldn't face that other fellow ever, but I did not implicate my admirer. That boy, whom I had identified, didn't confront me at all, and I never saw him around. He was invisible before and ever after.

I was approached by many during those years, but no one could gather much strength to get past his first visit with me at the hostel. One came to wish me on my birthday, another to wish me a happy new year, and the bravest one proposed to me the first time he met me! I still remember his features—he was from eastern UP, five feet or even shorter, very thin and dark, with a Hitler-like moustache. He was pumped up in the boy's hostel to proclaim his feelings to me! This was after they were all drunk and delirious. He, however, did gather his wits, and then reached the hostel somehow, and called my name and waited. Everyone wondered what he was doing at my hostel. I came down and stood in the lobby, perplexed. He was trying to stand straight with effort, holding a rose as if to balance his centre of gravity.

'I love you. I love you very much,' he said, quickly.

I kept staring at him, and I remember how he turned and left just like that. I rushed back to my room and cried, totally unnerved by this. Exams were just around the corner. The boy must have wanted to ruin my score by playing this prank, I thought, sniffling. He had proven his bravery to everyone, I thought. Everyone was having fun at the cost of my mental agony, and the thought of this pained me further. We couldn't speak to each other ever after this incident. We wouldn't have spoken anyway.

Another incident that happened during those days is still vivid in my mind. An elder brother of one of my batchmates visited her in the hostel. During those days, I was trying to make my way into that group of girls from Ghaziabad and wanted their approval and attention. The elder brother of this batchmate of mine was in his forties. He had brought us cake, ice cream, samosas and coke. He asked me if I would like a ride till the shop in his car. Unaware of his intentions, I quickly jumped into his car, a Maruti 800. This was my second ride in any car. First was on the day of my selection in medical college when we rode in Arora Uncle's car to the station. And then was this, the second ride, a shameful one. He started the car and instead of turning it towards our college campus gate that would lead to the shops or other busy areas, he drove to the other side, towards the dark, scary love lane. As we drove, we saw no streetlights, and there was absolutely no person in sight. The tall trees and thick bushes obscured the moonlight, and I started feeling a chill of fear down my spine.

As he slowed the car to a standstill, his hands started slipping down my thighs and up on my bust. I became numb in shock, I didn't have any energy to shout, and my throat went dry. I couldn't figure out what to do, or how to stop it. I wanted to get out of the car, and run away in the dark. I don't remember what I said or did at that moment, but I remember him taking a U-turn after a while.

I ran inside without paying any heed to the giggling girls spreading the delicacies on the cemented sitting area in the open space outside our hostel gate. No one came to check on me or invite me to partake of the treat; all I remember is that I kept waiting and crying, crying my heart out with dismay and shock. I was not a part of the group anyway; it was me who was trying against all odds to become their friend. I have lived with the unpleasant memories of that nauseating incident till date but have not been able to share it with anyone. There was no question of telling the parents; I knew they would feel miserable and helpless upon knowing it all. I also realised I would have to live with it since it had already happened, and no one could ever change it.

During the first year of medical college, it is really tormenting to wake up to the harsh realities of the world, as we are away from the protective cocoon of our homes. Ages later, as I am writing this when I am well into my forties, my throat is still choked. I didn't cry then; I couldn't. I want to release this burden now. As I aged, I have come to acknowledge that incidents like these are common with girls at any age. It toughens us.

The journey from the college to the city was a very long stretch. There were areas on that stretch without any streetlight, house or shops nearby, and in those areas, notorious boys would pass us, touching our chests, pulling our dupattas, patting our backs or thighs. We girls have been through these deplorable incidents of sexual harassment and survived.

As a girl, there have been plenty of incidents scattered across my hostel life where I have felt vulnerable. Once while bathing, I discovered some itchy rashes on my body, mostly on the tummy, naval, in between my fingers and underarms. The discomfort and itching became severe during the nights. As a first-year MBBS student, I tried Dettol, Savlon, Neem water, hot water bath and anti-allergic tablets, but to no avail. It kept spreading and became intensely pruritic, and uncomfortable. I was not able to study because of these itchy rashes. I was advised to go to the dermatologist, so I did. OPD was busy in general, so I kept waiting for my turn.

By the time, the doctor noticed me, it was lunch hour. He apologised and invited me to his house clinic. We went inside and then I showed him my rashes, which by then looked like water-filled tiny acnes on the ventral surface of my body, my hands, arms, underarms, below my breast and naval. These were typical rashes, in fact, now I know the diagnosis myself. It was a commonplace, contagious skin infection called scabies, seen in students living in hostels. There was only one treatment, a specific lotion to be applied below the neck area for three days, and it would vanish like magic.

He had diagnosed it immediately, as was expected. However, he called me into the examination room alone. My roommate frowned; we were not sure of anything. He asked to see my back. Now that we are doctors, we know that scabies never spreads to dorsal surfaces like back of arms or legs or the back. However, back then it was a mysterious, prickly disturbing disease to us. He felt my back slowly, measuring its curves. I couldn't understand why he was doing that. I withdrew myself, unsettled by his touch. He fumbled, retracted and composed himself quickly before facing me. Then he explained the treatment to us curtly and left the room without even showing us out.

During my tenure at the hostel, I also noticed some common and stray incidents which strengthened my knowledge about my college, and which later became part of my haunting memories.

In the boys' hostel, eastern UP boys were called TICKS—an abbreviation for 'Total Ignorance of Culture and Knowledge'. These boys at the hostel coming from eastern UP didn't know English; their etiquette in conversing with girls and their presentation was very poor, although they were better in overall studies and merit. The TICK-word was thrown at them in a very abusive manner.

There were some easy ways to get passing marks without studying. Being the cultural secretary and the sports secretary were two of the easy ways out. Some boys, by using their extracurricular skills like singing, became quite popular and well-known in senior circles. This, itself, taught me that life was about exploring new ventures and making the best out of them.

The murkiness of the adult world struck us too during our college days. We got to know that after the exams, the boys used to collect money to rent a VCR with porn movies and would help themselves into experiencing orgasmic pleasure multiple times while watching. A few of the bold ones pooled in their money and got a sex worker into the hostel to indulge in random, recurring sex for one whole night. However, the hapless girl ran for her life when a particular tall, dark and broad-shouldered boy approached her. The fellow was made fun of long after this incident.

Boys consumed ganja and gambled as well. Grinding endless medical literature demanded some recreation. Once a group of boys strolling back from gambling noticed a distressed man trying to start his bike vigorously. Humbled and ecstatic under the effect of ganja, all of them tried to help him only to find out later that he was a bike thief. The man stole one of their bikes and was almost beaten to death by the stoned gang once he was caught. Eventually, he coughed up the names of his gang members who were stealing bikes from the campus. The next day, many lost bikes were recovered.

Often, silent acts of infatuation towards a certain girl sparked conflicts amongst the boys. One such incident took a dangerous political turn and almost destroyed the future of several innocent bystanders. One day during class, while moving chairs to fit into the crammed space in one of the smaller lecture rooms, Tripathi accidentally banged into Nadira's chair. The girl was hot-tempered and was already irked by his awkward behaviour on many previous occasions.

She snapped at him in front of the whole class.

The news spread like wildfire and the next day, Abdul Ali, a day scholar beat Tripathi in front of everyone just after class ended. It was sudden and without any provocation, and Tripathi was caught off guard. The slaps, punches, and the pushing continued, and he was even pulled by the ear. He started bleeding from his nose, his eyes were bruised and there was blood flowing from his injured mouth. It all happened in a jiffy, and we didn't have any clue as to why he had to endure such brutal violence. Abdul left immediately after the bloodshed, and the class was cancelled. We heard whispering, conjecturing all around us as a few peers helped Tripathi to the first-aid room.

However, the brawl didn't end there; there was more to the show. After a couple of days, Abdul tried to attack Tripathi again. This time, he was accompanied by local thugs and a few more boys from his community. They came with chains and hockey sticks. The fight between the two groups, led to serious injuries to a boy, who was the son of a local politician. Unfortunately, a simple local tiff had turned into a political feud, and had taken on a communal hue. Multiple summons and court hearings for the Tripathi group boys were followed by an 'out of court' settlement and apologies. It took a toll on their studies, and caused them a lot of mental agony. The incident was an eye-opener to me in many respects and taught me that simple things could snowball into very big, disastrous events if they weren't checked on time.

Field Posting and Practical Experience

MY FIRST village posting is still fresh in my memory. I was assigned the practice of Social and Preventive Medicine. We were divided into groups of twenty students each and were given responsibility of villages under our PHC (primary health centre).

We were brought to this village in a medical college bus for our field duty. The group was very excited about the field posting, as it was kind of like a picnic for us young girls and boys in our twenties. As soon as the bus dropped us off in front of a vast yellow mustard field, we were led to the village by a path through the field. The path meandered around wells, big Banyan trees, brick structures with cow dung filled till the top, and machines to cut the crop.

I remembered walking for a kilometre along with others to reach a cluster of houses. There was a narrow-tiled road between rows of dissimilar houses—some big, some small, some with tin roofs, some with brick. I remembered the wooden door and an iron gate, a well and a tractor, a tree with a parapet around it, an open area, a building with a row of small rooms with faded words written on the front facing wall of a senior secondary school. We were gathered near the Banyan tree, divided into groups of three.

Each group was assigned one family, instructed to educate them about *kuccha* house, *pucca* house, drainage system, latrines, garbage collection and disposal, health and good nutrition among other things.

I remember the half-naked kids staring at us in awe and curiosity. Women working in their makeshift kitchens on mud *chulha* (stove) were amused to see us in our white doctor coats, chirping and jumping around. We were enjoying the out-station trip away from our usual dose of microbiology, pharmacology, and of examining mutilated bodies from mortuaries and looking at forensic and microscopic slides of diseased organs.

The villagers watched us apprehensively, as if we were foreigners who were encroaching on their territory. We remained oblivious, happy with ourselves.

As MBBS students, we were ignorant about the challenges of private practice, our upcoming competition with quacks or with the pathetic state of government-run primary health care centres in villages.

It was the month of Ramzan when we explored the village as part of our medical assignment. The village women were busy cooking an elaborate evening meal to break their fast. The aroma filled our nostrils. Some of us joined the ladies working on mud *chulhas* in their front yards. We started peeling potatoes, talking about what was on the menu. A few girls sneaked out with their boyfriends to secret hideouts, for intense kissing sessions. Other boisterous boys went around

with our instructors, the postgraduate students in PSM. They wanted to have fun and leave. None of us wanted to count kuccha latrines, pucca latrines, shallow or deep wells, or check the state of drinking water and sanitation. None of us wanted to preach to the village natives about the importance of antenatal classes, contraception, or immunisation awareness programmes.

Looking back, I also remember the time of our first hospital posting. The head of the department met the new doctors of the future. He was a confident personality in his early fifties, surrounded by consultants, senior residents, postgraduate students, and us undergraduates thronging the patient's bedside.

I vividly remember him asking us to take a case history of this patient and present it in fifteen minutes to him. All twenty-five of us started at our first case. How to make a note of the history?

We opened the book. One read aloud to help others; some studious loners shushed us to read it alone with concentration. We read it all—chief complaints of the patient, duration and history of present illness, history of surgery, prolonged illness, history of drug allergies, family history etc.

I still remember how frustrated the HOD was when he asked us to present the case. All of us were asking different questions to the patient. Sometimes the same question was asked multiple times, and yet the patient was cooperating. He didn't seem irritated and was amused. No one had noted down the history, methodically. No one dared to now face the head of surgery without systematic preparation. We stood with our heads bowed in shame.

'Until you present the history, we are not going to start examining the patient. Noting the patient's history is an art, and through it, you can extract elaborate information about the patient's disease,' I remember him saying this.

After recording a patient's history, we learnt about clinical examination, followed by making a differential diagnosis, with supporting investigations, followed by a final diagnosis, and disease management. We got better with time, and with practice.

After a few months, we could take one case each, independently. An individual patient was always a 'case' for us. A lump in the abdomen, firm to hard, mobile, tender to touch, warm. We examined the lump multiple times to get the proper feel before case presentation. Hundreds of students examined the same patient every day. It was a lump. Yet its attachment to the human body, its pain or distress, could never be understood by us. We were only interested in the lump's origin, its consistency, the management and prognosis after treatment.

In case of heart patients with shortness of breath, we couldn't feel their agony though we were noticing it, writing it down in our notes.

Medical college patients seemed to be very patient and tolerant. We hurt them with repeated poking, without sensing their helplessness or pain. Though they were treated well, diagnosis was always made by postgraduate students. For us, the undergraduate students, they were just 'cases,' an abdominal lump, a murmur, pyrexia (fever) of unknown origin, etc. At other times, we were more interested in love relationships sprouting between postgraduate boys and undergraduate girls.

The one beautiful thing that came out of all this was the way UG-PG bonds were becoming stronger. We helped one another, supported in PG entrance examination, prepared them for viva, did combined studies. Inter-batch or intra-batch affairs were common, and I have vivid recollections of their involvements and how they used to be a world by themselves.

During those days, no one admitted that they studied, and by nine most of the lights were out and the doors closed. Behind the closed doors, we studied with lamp lights to hide our toil. It didn't matter though, because in medical college, one just needed to pass the exam; no one cared about percentage in the MBBS degree.

As juniors, our duties were to prepare notes, complete the manuals for our seniors while they were busy in their love affairs, offer them warm tea at wee hours, wake them up in the middle of the night, or read aloud to our sleepy seniors when they were too tired to focus. It was all studies—twenty hours a day—mugging up thick books, line by line, making notes, presentations, manuals, reading about instruments, organ specimens, pathology and histopathology slides under microscope, viva questions, laboratory booklets. As many as close to thirty books, sentences and pictures floated around our young brains. While sleeping or awake, in our dreams, we could only visualise dead organs, creepy organisms, and, of course, our notes.

Till the age of thirty-five or maybe even later, I would wake up from nightmares. I dreamt and lived my failure in the exams, going blank while looking at the question paper hundreds of times. I remember writing a beautiful, detailed essay on mitral regurgitation while the question was on mitral stenosis. The blunder that I committed on the question of rickettsia was also worth remembering. Third year subjects were boring to the hilt. But my studious batchmates were busy mugging everything up.

When it all came to an end, I realised it was worth it. Except for two students, all of us cleared the final year exams of MBBS. Out of 110 students, 108 became doctors. Five years of constant studies, running between college, hostel, and hospital, sitting long hours in the library, had finally come to an end. Hours of making tea, eating Maggi, trying to keep our eyes open forcibly, absorbing yet another topic in our overloaded brains, reading about tons of diseases and their causes, drugs, and disease management, surviving on canteen food, *lassi* from a stall outside the hostel gate, making STD calls from a telephone booth at 5 am or 10 pm, taking multiple rounds at labs to revise the specimens and slides—all of it came to an end.

We were doctors now. It was an overwhelming experience!

Now what? What next? How did we go about treating patients? We knew about insertion and origin of muscles, articulation of joints, nerve supply and vessels, types of ulcers, heart sounds and murmurs, about tumours and their origins, consistency, margins, and diagnosis. We knew all the microbiology and pathology; we knew the tests to determine which bacteria or parasite could have caused the respective diseases. We knew all the drugs, their actions, side-effects and dosages. But we were unable to connect those subjects to real-time cases.

Had we wasted our five years in medical studies, we wondered.

Did we waste our time, staying away from home, struggling each day, fighting hostel politics, studying, learning, making friends and foes, enjoying extracurricular activities, picnics, and parties? I remember how homesick we all felt during our first year. Together, we wanted to flee from the tremendous stress without the comforting company of childhood friends and family. We bunked college (the whole batch did it) every twenty-fifth day of the month. It used to be mass bunking. It took us long to adjust to harsh hostel life.

But now, after our MBBS degree, patients were waiting for us to treat them and answer their medical queries. Unfortunately, we as doctors were clueless. What was the brand name of Ranitidine, metformin, diclofenac, or paracetamol? We didn't have any idea. We knew about the theoretical part—anatomy, pathology, physiology, microorganisms, disease presentation, differential diagnosis, and management, but what about their clinical application?

At first, we felt dizzy, almost light-headed with these questions, but gradually, the burden of it all turned into a noose, straining at our necks. We were doctors without practical knowledge. I shared the question of our limitations as doctors with one of my seniors on receiving her praise on my result. She laughed and shared her insights.

She reminded me that during our compulsory one-year internship, we would learn practical medicine. She reminded me that we already had first-hand experience with patient handling, and would soon become aces at withdrawing blood for lab work, putting cannula, inserting catheters, reading ECG and X-ray, venesection, drawing ABG, spinal tap, simple suturing, dressing, removing sutures, treating cardiac arrest, burn cases, also dealing with tetanus poisoning, trauma etc. She pointed out that we had already received wide clinical exposure and realised where our interest lay in terms of specialisation.

Postgraduation is the time to learn in depth about that single speciality, i.e. gynae, paediatrics, surgery or whatever one gets to choose through his or her merit in the PG entrance exam.

Also, in our internship village postings, we learnt how to diagnose and manage patients independently from senior doctors. And true, we became clinicians after a year of compulsory internship.

Thinking of my own village posting as an intern, I was assigned a deserted one room, isolated from the village, somewhere in the middle of a field near a big Neem tree. Without a working ceiling fan, the only breeze was the warm air, tempered with the cool breeze that blew in from the Neem tree. As a practising doctor in the village, the main problem I encountered was the scarcity of patients. As the availability of doctors was not consistent, the villagers lost interest. Also, they couldn't afford to wait for long hours in the hospital, neglecting their field jobs and their cattle.

A Doctor at Last!

THE DAY of the result was monumental. We all passed. We were now firmly on the path towards becoming doctors. All along we'd been circling around the axis of studying, fighting, working in the lab, and presenting cases. But now we were free to leave our orbit. This sudden feeling of zero gravity felt uneasy.

We needed to collect our results from Lucknow Medical College, after which we had to start our internship—one mandatory year of practice in the hospital. Medicine practice encompassed every speciality—from emergency medicine to gynaecology, surgery, ophthalmology, paediatrics, medicine, orthopaedics, and preventive and social medicine, for which we would have to work in a village hospital. It was an interesting year. We learnt complicated medical procedures.

We learnt the hierarchical procedures the hard way and were happy that our theoretical knowledge was utilised effectively in the practical setting of the hospital. During internship, we learnt many new lessons while on the job, much more than we got to learn as postgraduate students.

As the days passed by, our focus changed from Master of Medicine and Surgery to a specific subject. From gaining a broader vision, we gradually moved to a microscopic vision. Once we were in practice, we gradually gained confidence in small lifesaving ER procedures. Those days, we had a compulsory six-month village posting, including a mandatory few months working with a PHC or CHC.

Attending the PHC clinic at a village panchayat with no logistical support, medicines, instruments, light, proper sitting or examination area was an unsurmountable challenge for us all. At that level, as the juniormost members in the medical chain, our wish to reform things was never granted. Moreover, we realised that we could bunk, proxy or just vanish from our PHC posting to study for our postgraduate entrance exam, which was another mammoth task.

At this crucial juncture of my life, a sudden decision to marry me off was taken by my parents, which altered the course of my life.

Marriage and My Little Angel

AS I was the eldest amongst three daughters in our family, it was time for our parents to start marrying each one off as soon as we had started to enter our twenties. On turning twenty-one, suitable matches were sought for me on a regular basis. I rejected many proposals, as I was not in sync with the plan. My father requested me to reconsider my decision once he found a perfect match, a wealthy, but humble, homely family. The cherry on top of the cake was their boy—tall, fair, handsome, and pursuing postgraduation in Paediatrics from a government medical college. I met the boy, and he looked like the hero Arvind Swamy from South Indian movies, with a thick moustache. I was more than willing after meeting the family and seeing him from the window furtively. My resistance to marry flew out of the window as I was swooning over the boy's charming looks.

Instead of Gorakhpur where I was studying for my MBBS, I chose to do my internship in another north Indian state where I would be staying after marriage. I had got married just after my MBBS results were declared. My roommate was upset—she had wanted both of us to be together till we finished studying for our postgraduation entrance exams.

She felt I was cheating her, leaving my study mate midway, and she also maintained that my own career was at stake, that it was a foolish decision of mine to marry at this point. She said I was ruining her life too, and that I would never clear the entrance exam if marriage spoiled the momentum of studies, and that I was selfish to leave her to her fate.

She was right. Marriage transforms life.

Along with my duties as an intern, I was expected to do household chores like cooking, among many other things. My husband planned to buy a house outside the campus to live like a proper couple, with a bedroom, kitchen, and a living space to accommodate guests, but I was not in sync with this plan.

In the early months of our marriage, we were living in the hostel, eating from the mess, washing our clothes with laundry services. There were no guests we could attend to, only study, and perform my hospital duties till I secured my postgraduate seat. It was an uncomfortable situation for him, a traditional man with an orthodox upbringing. It went my way, so I believed. We stayed in the hostel for my studies. Studying alone in a different environment with no study mate to compete with and with no discussions to participate in, I felt that I would soon lose my will to study.

A few days later, when I missed my periods, I had mixed reactions and wasn't sure how to process the news. The day we confirmed the news, we were very happy to see two red lines on my urine pregnancy kit. I was floating in the air, my feet off the ground, a smile plastered on my face. My husband and I were emotional about starting a family. Holding each other's

hands, we celebrated the news with our family over a phone call. Everybody was jubilant to receive the news. However, within a few days, it struck me that it might not be good news after all! How was I going to study or give my exams after the delivery? Would I be able to join the college after the baby was born?

The bodily changes during my pregnancy became immensely challenging, especially in the first trimester. With intermittent puking, acidity and constipation, the struggle got difficult every day. I was not able to sit for long, get up or turn on the bed by myself. Moreover, I was studying twenty hours a day, and not eating enough partly because I didn't feel much appetite and eating would make me sluggish and drowsy. Sometime later, further tests revealed that the baby inside me was not gaining weight due to intrauterine growth restrictions. The fact that the baby was not growing enough didn't help my will to eat or sleep either. Digestion was a constant problem and lying down in the afternoon for a couple of hours was not possible with the unimaginable academic burdens that the medical fraternity has to bear.

There was still an immeasurable amount of study material to cover before the entrance tests, and with my ill health, I didn't know what fate awaited me.

Hospital duties during the day, library hours in between and continuous studies throughout the night with only few hours of sleep was my daily routine, and I was trying hard to get accustomed to it. My PG entrance exam, which was supposed to take place in UP, was just a few months away, followed by the all India PG exams and Manipal. I was afraid that my roommate was right, I wouldn't be able to compete, and my career would come to a grinding halt. I wanted to prove myself, not because of her negative words, but for my own sake. I wanted to be a doctor worth her degree; I craved to be a practising super specialist. My ultimate dream was only a few exams away; I didn't want to lose my focus.

However, my results weren't satisfactory. All my batchmates got the seats as per their interests, but I didn't. I was in the waiting list again. Shattered, humiliated by my roommate's grim predictions for my future, I started preparing for Manipal, the last exam left for that year.

I was in my eighth month of pregnancy and despite my delicate physical condition, we flew to Mangalore to write the exam. The exam, however, didn't go as per my expectations, and I had a feeling I wouldn't make it.

Nonetheless, we enjoyed South Indian food, bought the famous Mangalorean silk sarees, and my father's colleague in Oriental Insurance Company took great care of us during our stay there. My father's reputation as an easy-going, flexible, humorous, and honest audit officer was well known to all, which explained why they were so welcoming in their hospitality. His reputation as a generous and humanitarian officer helped us and was reflected in the warmth we received in Mangalore.

However, after the exams were over, we came back, and I had to continue with my internship. The results were to be announced in one month, and I knew I would have delivered the baby by then.

I was only praying that the delivery date shouldn't fall on the same date as my counselling.

I remember the day I went into labour very vividly. It was a difficult labour that lasted for more than twenty hours

starting at 11 am on 20 September till 7 am the next day. I was exhausted with its nightmarish impact.

The descending head of the baby tears the mother's pelvic bones apart. I was shouting with pain, begging the doctors attending to me to do a Caesarean section, but my guardians were deciding the mode of delivery. It was not in my control. I was left in that government labour room alone to accept my pains and live with it. My screams were ignored, my husband was not allowed to come inside.

The resident doctor who visited to examine me for the dilation muttered, 'It's just 2-3 centimetres. It takes 12-14 hours from here to full dilatation, followed by delivery.'

I was writhing in excruciating pain, my hip bones were cracking, as if someone was pulling my legs from both the sides and trying to rip me apart.

Is this the way women deliver everyday around the world, I wondered, in the midst of my excruciating pain that if this is a fact, then why am I not able to take it? It was beyond my understanding. I wanted to die, and I was sure I would die of the shock of birth pangs any moment. I turned to the other side, forcing my mouth shut, swallowing each contraction with silence till the next morning. By then, I had literally lost track of time. I lay in hibernation, quiet, flexing my muscles, but still resilient.

'I will overcome this,' I vowed to myself.

The resident doctors kept coming to check the progress every four hours. I kept quiet. In these quiet moments of suffering, my partner was not there to support me, and this was inscribed somewhere in my consciousness. Around 7 o'clock in the morning, when the shift was changing, I was fully dilated. That was not an appropriate time for delivery. Everyone wanted to rush home and push the remaining cases to the people on the new shift. The morning staff wanted the night staff to perform the delivery if it was due from the previous night. Night staff was too tired and desired to sign off. As for myself, I was dying to push out the baby, but there was no one in sight. After a while, some commotion could be heard from a distance.

'Head is at the perineum,' I could hear a voice shouting. All the staff on duty gathered around; the senior consultant was called. Suddenly, I felt as if all the pain, all the agony of my contractions disappeared.

'Push, push, Anu, we can see the head of the baby, push it out hard,' the voices shouted in unison.

But strangely enough, the urge of pushing wasn't there in my body. No pain, no agony, only an endless exhaustion. I was tired, weary, and lost. After such long hours of continued pain, all my senses were blunted. My tired ears were hearing all the voices around, but I couldn't respond. The consultant doctor's patience wore off. She took the call to apply vacuum on the crowning head of the baby to pull it out of my pelvis. Everyone shouted in chorus again.

'Anu, push with this contraction! Or else the baby will be pulled out with instruments,' they said.

My brain was too tired to respond, and there seemed to be a total disconnect between the mind and the body. Whatever it was, I totally failed to push. The night staff was restless, tired after the ordeal of the entire night. They were dying to go home right after this delivery.

After a while of waiting, vacuum was applied with the

consensus of the senior consultant doctor and all the staff. As for myself, I have a very fizzy memory of the surroundings during this moment. Everyone changed into their normal clothes, ready to run as soon as the baby was out.

They needed to go home after this daily routine as endless chores awaited them at home. Kids needed to be kissed and sent to school, household errands needed to be finished. After the last warning to me, they were ready to bring out the baby by applying the vacuum. I was disconnected. I tried hard to muster whatever strength was left in me but couldn't gather any, as neither my brain nor my body was in my control. And the baby was pulled with the force of a vacuum. It was a tiny baby girl, all of 2.45 kgs. The baby cried within a few seconds and was immediately handed over to the paediatrician. Someone was at my perineum stitching me up and removing my placenta. When I think of it all today, some random scenes come back as vague memories.

But I remember holding in my arms, my tiny, delicate girl. She was a part of my flesh, my own blood. The instantaneous connect, my sudden transformation into being a mother seemed unbelievable. That ambitious girl inside me died in those excruciating hours of my labour pains. This tiny wonder was such a beauty. It was mine, and only mine. I wouldn't let anyone hurt her ever. She seemed so dependent on me. I was her world, her nurturer, her provider, and protector. I said to myself repeatedly that she was my responsibility. I could not leave her out of my sight even for a second, I thought. I was overwhelmed. I was now a mother, and the word held its own weight.

When I came back home with my tiny bundle of joy, she became my world. I couldn't think of anything beyond her.

Nor could I trust anyone with her. No one could hold her properly, not even my parents. No one could comfort her. I wanted her to be with me, clinging to me every second. All chores of the baby—including breastfeeding, bathing, or cleaning were handled by me singlehandedly. I was paranoid for her safety, her comfort, tending to her every little need, admiring her each passing minute. I was sleepless for days together because no one knew how to feed her. I kept cradling her, feeding her, taking care of her as if an invisible umbilical cord still connected us.

I was so immersed in taking care of my daughter, I forgot about my Manipal exam's result.

The result in the form of a thick booklet was received by speed post after fifteen days of my delivery. On the first page my score was amongst the first fifty. The news sounded unbelievable. I was invited for counselling on a particular date, and failing to appear there would result in striking off my name from the list. We understood that under such circumstances, the seat would be awarded to the next candidate in line. But after my delivery, I didn't want to do PG right away, I was determined nothing could separate me from my daughter. She was a fragile, delicate infant, and there was no question of leaving her alone with anybody, not even my parents.

Everyone tried to counsel me, reminded me of my dream to be a postgraduate doctor. Everyone in my family congratulated me for the brilliant score and persuaded me to go for counselling to fetch a seat in a good stream, a surgical speciality as I had always wanted for myself. However, it was unimaginable, and the timing was just not right. I knew even if I picked a course, I would not join it. It was not possible to

leave my child for the sake of PG.

However, with everyone's persistence, finally we booked the ticket to Mangalore, and then drove in a taxi to Udupi. Everything had been arranged by my father. I was so proud of him.

The choices were laid out in front of me—Obstetrics and Gynae, second last seat, General Surgery last seat, DMRD; Radiology, and all other branches except Medicine and Skin. I could choose a three-year degree course in any subject of my interest. Students were waiting in the hall, with their eyes glued to the display screen to check which seat was gone, and what were the options they still had, to choose from. My future was one tick away at that moment. I collected myself—a mother, a daughter, a pragmatic visionary. I picked a three-year degree course in OBGYN.

It was a great moment that defined my life in many ways. All my friends had got their PG seat. Without postgraduate, one is not considered an efficient doctor. It's a prevalent belief, a norm that is understandable. You have much deeper knowledge of the subject, a mastery in that speciality after the PG course. Today when I look back, I believe that day opened the door to my academic accomplishments and my career.

As soon as I filled my option, my identity card was printed, laminated and handed over to me. I was told to join the college in fifteen days' time. Now that was quick, I thought. I was part of the institute instantaneously. Brochures, hostel list, and a bunch of other information were handed over to me in a nice, labelled file, titled MD OBGYN Dr Anu.

It was exhilarating, if only I could join, I heard my heart say to myself. It wasn't possible to leave my baby daughter just like that. She was just an infant! Was there any room for confusion now that I had given birth to her? I could not put these two totally contrasting choices on a scale. But why was it paradoxical? Was I still not a girl who wanted to go ahead and grasp her dream? How could motherhood hinder me from attaining my dreams? Was it possible for me to pursue my passion as well as raise a child?

But luck was on my side. The Counsellor heard me out and realised how important my new role as a mother was to me. I was given six months' grace and was allowed to join my postgraduation studies with the next batch! I breathed a sigh of relief. I could be with my baby girl for a few months.

Postgraduation and a Labour Case that Haunts till Today

I CHOSE Mangalore Medical College for my postgraduation, at Lady Grace Hospital. It was a colonial building with a good broad gate, a fairly good area for parking, and a huge entrance to the reception, as well as a centre desk behind which there was an old, black phone with the old ring dial system. I remember the receptionist who would make entries and guide the patients to a grand hall or the OPD hall—a huge single room with three tables in the centre. It had four examination rooms, one big room for senior consultants to rest in during their tea and coffee breaks, and one more rectangular hall at the far-left end. This hall was not functional on a regular basis, and even if it was, we were not aware of its function.

That hall at the far-left end of the OPD hall, the corridor leading to the hospital building, and the large green area in that colonial building, previously a manicured garden, had haunted me since long. I still remember the huge hall, lined by beds in three horizontal rows, with a row of beds placed against each wall. Straight ahead was the room of the doctor on duty, so, after two beds there was no space to stand. And on walking ahead, we discovered a door in the wall of the hall, which led to the high-risk labour ward.

The big ward had four labour beds, and the nurses' desk was inside. I didn't see the sign of the 'Doctor's Desk' above the door, as it was blackened with mould and rust for more than sixty years. We looked at the old beds, the ancient, lumpy and sagging mattresses, and the wide windows, devoid of any curtains, overlooking the green patch outside.

Ahead was a long corridor, laced with rows of beds with patients, leading to another hall. This was the low-risk labour ward. Beside this was the low-risk labour room, a sitting area surrounded by five labour beds. Before entering the labour room, I could see a staircase leading to the first floor, paediatrics ward, and second floor paediatrics NICU ward. I still remember how awed I was by the beautiful structure of the corridor, bordered by green patches on either side. The vintage building bore testimony to the meticulous design of the colonial era.

There were three wards in total, one for post-delivered patients, another for post-operative patients, and one more for pre-operative gynae patients—the poor, underprivileged ones suffering from prolapse uterus, cancer cervix or uterus—awaiting their turn for surgery.

It was a government-run hospital aided by private institutions. Private medical college students were running the hospital services, and their consultants were guiding them in the labour room and OT. Government doctors didn't have much role there. They would come and go as they pleased. For some reason, they were perpetually angry with students, either because the students were from private institutes or

because they had no authority left in the system to run the show. Whatever was the case, we could sense and feel the strain during our accidental encounters with them, while our consultants were busy practitioners, on the payroll of this private medical college. They were busy with their private practice and had no time except for a flying visit once a week. They had good knowledge, and were masters of surgery, but they lacked in their intent and attitude.

Since, we were made to work so much, none of us felt any sense of belonging to the place. The government as well as the medical college authorities couldn't care less about how things kept moving either. As a result, this beautiful building was rotting for almost sixty years. The vacant green area was a breeding ground for mosquitoes. Moreover, because Mangalore was a coastal region with constant rainfall, patients in every ward were affected with malaria and were dying. The germs of malaria *vivax, falciparum*—all would breed leisurely in the dirty ponds, or giant puddles that would form on both sides of the corridors, following fresh bouts of rain.

I remember how I had to see vast number of patients with only textbook knowledge of the disease, something that I had never done before. Pregnant patients were admitted for the management of pregnancy induced hypertension, for follow up of bad obstetric history, while malaria was served to them literally on a platter. More than eighty per cent admissions in the ward contracted malarial parasitic infection. High grade fever with chills, every 48-72 hours, night sweats, vomiting, diarrhoea, headache, cough, and shivering were the symptoms we anticipated in every admitted patient, but we were ready with chloroquine.

It's hard to believe now that we offered it as a prophylactic drug to patients, because we were so sure of them getting malaria after admission. The drug itself was a torture, giving severe acidity and vomiting to the patients. I remember seeing patients deteriorating into cerebral malaria for the first time, becoming drowsy, unconscious, slipping into coma due to clotting of brain vessels. Our patients were usually from among the utterly poor, uneducated labour class.

Our educated, rich consultants were aware, and we as young resident doctors were aware of why it was happening, and how to avoid it. Instead, we were learning how to manage mild, moderate or severe forms of malaria. We were taking care of treatment protocols, in case of patients with pulmonary symptoms, pregnant and lactating mothers. We were managing multidrug resistant strains, prescribing different drugs for different parasites such as *vivax, falciparum.*

We were learning how to differentiate them from symptoms and signs. We never went to the hospital without applying mosquito repellent cream. It was a permanent home to mosquitos since years, and we were temporary foreigners.

Such a discrepancy in our medical system has remained since years, and being doctors, we were at the receiving end of it all. We couldn't change the system back then; we can't change the system even now.

Labour room postings were the most fun part of post-graduate training. The labour rooms were considered the most happening places, with continuous flow of pregnant patients in different weeks of gestation, with different complaints ranging from early pregnancy loss, mid-pregnancy contractions, preterm labour or leaking, and full-term

pregnancies with malpresentation (baby with feet coming first or hand protruding through vagina).

Ladies with full-term pregnancies who had their baby's head down towards their vaginas were directed to LR and women with high BP, high sugar, fever, abnormal vaginal bleeding early in pregnancy, and many more varieties of complicated cases were directed to high risk LR. High risk LR was quite taxing to one's psyche, so various techniques were utilised to manage seizures in patients during their deliveries. There were special techniques used for delivering a baby by feet (breech presentation) following manoeuvring as per guidelines.

The wards were always full of patients having bad obstetric history, malaria, pregnancy induced hypertension, and patients with other infectious diseases.

On the other hand, LR was kind of a factory for Caesarean deliveries.

In the low-risk labour room, though patients kept delivering every now and then. It was an easy duty, where we had more time to sit and chat, plan dinner, and get togethers. Patients came in at different stages of their labour. We treated patients for various problems—augmentation of contractions, bowel cleansing with enema, drugs for easy dilation of the cervix, the mouth of the uterus, perineal part preparation, test dose for local anaesthesia, antibiotics and so on.

We sat with paediatricians at the doctor's table, finishing our notes after examining patients and relied on nurses to carry out drug orders. We were interrupted from our daily banter with the doctors every now and then to deliver labouring women. Delivering the babies, handing them over to the paediatrician, suturing episiotomy and other such chores were all part of our daily routine.

Some days, we found ourselves too busy to breathe in the labour room. It was the same with the paediatric department. Paediatrics admissions were periodically on the rise due to the endemics in the region, including malaria, dengue, Japanese Encephalitis, and diarrhoea.

Some days the paediatric resident was not able to attend a normal vaginal delivery, hence we did resuscitation of the newborn. Our tasks included cleaning and rubbing the baby's back, stimulating it to cry, giving oxygen support with mask, suctioning its secretions in the mouth and upper throat, then wrapping the newborn in a warm clean towel before transferring it to the mother for breast feeding. As the deliveries were smooth and uncomplicated most of the times, no one raised a question as to why the paediatrician had not appeared for the delivery.

Primi: The Labour Case

One such morning, while we were sitting after rounds, one primi (first time pregnant) in labour and two other patients came to our hospital. The primi had been in labour since last night and was almost fully dilated and ready for delivery in an hour or so. We were waiting for the baby's head to descend, for the crowning to happen. Two hours passed, its head was high still; the pushing efforts of the mother were not enough. My senior advised to pull the baby out with vacuum with a cup-shaped device applied to the infant's head. A suction pressure is created on the baby's scalp and pulling it outside with force is not an uncommon practice during deliveries.

However, many times, this leads to internal bleeding in the baby's brain and vaginal lacerations to the mother. Hence, it is important that vacuum should be applied tactfully at the time of crowning with a gentle, single pull, only when the mother is exhausted and is not left with enough strength, due to prolonged labour.

We had learnt that if the baby's head seems to be high up in the vagina, we should refrain from doing it at all, as too much pressure from the pulling can be disastrous to the baby's brain and development.

The baby's head was still high, but the mother's cervix was fully dilated, so we were tempted to pull out the elongated crowned part of the head of the baby. But for a while we refrained because resident doctors are often blamed for not being able to differentiate between an obstructed labour which requires Caesarian section from a normal one. Consultants were aware that sometimes we would do vacuum or forceps delivery just for practice.

We tried pulling the baby through the head twice, but failed. Then my senior pulled it out with forceps extraction, a very difficult process. When the baby came out, its face was bruised with forceps marks, which would be handled later, but the immediate crisis was that the baby was not crying. Moreover, the paediatrician wasn't around. Calls were sent twice, but no one came down from the second-floor NICU (nursery). No class four worker was around to send the call again.

At that very moment, my senior started resuscitation on the baby, rubbing the baby's back, applying suction and oxygen. The baby lay limp; we checked its heart rate. It showed 90-100. I held the baby in my arms, snuggling it to my chest and ran upstairs to the second-floor nursery at the end of the corridor. I ran with all my might. It was a healthy 3.8 kg baby, and it needed to be saved. Only the paediatricians could save the newborn.

'They will intubate it and all will be good. Why the hell didn't they come for the delivery?' I said to myself while rushing to the nursery.

The paediatric resident took over, tried everything possible, but to no avail. The newborn lay limp, dying of internal brain bleeding owing to vacuum and forceps (instrumental) delivery.

I cried a lot that day. The baby could've been saved if the paediatric resident had resuscitated it immediately or if we had done a C-section instead of vacuum-assisted vaginal delivery. But like many medical blunders I have witnessed in my life, this was another blunder which would haunt me forever.

Gestational Diabetes Mellitus

IN THE postgraduate degree course, a thesis or research topic had to be selected and approved by our consultant guide. We needed to do a case control study on that topic during our tenure, analyse our collected data and make a presentation on multiple factors in the form of flow charts, tables, and graphs to make it easy to understand.

Twenty-five years ago, my senior had selected for me a case study and analysis of the prevalence and effects of Gestational Diabetes Mellitus in pregnancy. We were asked to test every pregnant female at around twenty-four weeks or later to diagnose if she was going to develop GDM.

The test was simple—75 gm glucose had to be taken with water within fifteen minutes, and after two hours, blood sugar was to be tested. If the value came higher than 140 mg/dl, the diagnosis was that she was prone to develop GDM. The material was distributed to OPDs, labour rooms, and IPD wards. We needed at least twenty-five cases for statistical calculations. However, by the end of one year, the entire hospital could detect only two such cases. What was the reason?

We could find out that while in the west, GDM was a common occurrence, here we couldn't even get enough cases to move our study further. As we all know, diabetes is a disease that originates from disorders in our daily lifestyle. But back then in a government hospital setting, where the labour class comprised most of the patients, chances of finding patients with diabetes were bleak. It was a common occurrence among the wealthier class, with their lethargic lifestyle, in which they did no physical work. After wasting one year, she had to change my topic for the case study.

Now after so many years, in my practice, I perform routine testing of GDM with the glucose challenge test. And as expected, more than thirty per cent cases are at risk of GDM. Online jobs performed while sitting in a single place, with minimal or no movement at all, no physical activity outside of work, instant food, a low-fibre simple carbohydrate diet, juices, soups, cheese as calcium supplement, bakery products, restaurant and processed food available at any time of the day are the main causes of GDM.

Most pregnant females start their pregnancy with high BMI, gaining 20-25 kg instead of 8-13 kg calculated as per their BMI. Many have essential hypertension at the age of thirty, others have hypothyroidism or insulin resistance. It gives me immense pain and discomfort to witness such deterioration of health among my patients in recent years, most of which can be avoided if they modify their lifestyle.

The Day I Forgot to Scrub

I WAS in my first year PG training. We were like interns, suddenly promoted to the status of residents without much knowledge of the OT or OPD, the protocols, or behavioural guidelines.

During our PG training, we got to know that the head nurse everywhere is the most honourable person in this territory. Even the head of the department fears her and shows her respect. She keeps the OT running, takes care of the inventory of anaesthesia drugs, washed and sterile-packed instruments and ensures a steady supply of sterile OT linen, cleaned and autoclaved scrubs, checks the duty scheduling of the OT staff, checks files for consent and site of operation, sends tissue samples for histopathology testing, and does other daily chores to keep the OT running smoothly. The OT duties would start sharp at 8 am, and with the packed schedule at the OT every day, it was the responsibility of the OT nurse to keep the routine running rhythmically.

We were terrified of the in-charge and her words were always final. If she said any of us was wrong, we had to

apologise and promise not to repeat our errors.

'Don't bother if she is wrong because consultants are not going to contradict her,' we would tell ourselves. However, if you had a great reputation with her, the journey at the OT would be as smooth as butter. She would make sure you were portrayed as the most hard-working and gifted surgeon. Consultants believed her recommendations and you would become a great surgeon by getting precious chances to scrub as first assistant to the senior surgeon.

My first scrubbing experience is something I remember till date. I learnt my glove size was six and a half. The nurse in-charge said hello and was instructing me every now and then in between her other supervisory jobs. For small cases like fallopian tube ligation or sterilisation surgery, MTP, abscess drainage etc, we didn't have a scrub nurse for assistance with our instruments. So, after scrubbing, we would proceed with our usual chores.

Our job was to count the instruments, inform the floor nurse to note it all down on the board, ask for betadine to paint the surgical area, drape it with sterile drapes, apply local anaesthetic drugs to the area of the surgical scar, wait for it to work, and then wait for our senior to start the case. My second-year senior was occupied with the next case in the list, so I was trying to put things in order before the senior consultant arrived.

I was waiting after scrubbing, not sure if I should go ahead and start the next thing. I was nervous. The instrument trolley was there with drapes on it. The nurse-in-charge told me to go ahead and start the case. It was a huge thing. I could envision cutting the skin, layer by layer, imagining which layer would

be after skin, subcutaneous fat, and then the rictus sheath, the toughest layer followed by rectus muscle and abdominal peritoneum, the deeper layer. But how to open the peritoneum?

I had observed clippings from the surgeries which I witnessed during the last couple of weeks, so I was kind of sure what to do. I draped the patient slowly, covered her legs and upper body, exposing only the surgical site.

My senior came and said, 'So are you ready for your first cut?'

I nodded.

'Hey, did you scrub the abdomen? The betadine bowl seems untouched,' he remarked.

No, oh my God. I forgot to scrub. I had been so preoccupied with my thoughts as to how to start the surgery, that I had draped her directly, without scrubbing. Right then, our HOD from the government hospital entered the OT. Ours was a minor OT, only for small procedures—like medical termination of pregnancy, sterilisation operations and Bartholin abscess drainage.

As we already know by now, government consultants hated us; we were from a private medical school and according to them, we were 'useless'. We didn't study hard; we were not fit for the dedication and diligence the medical profession required. She hated all of us, some a little more and others a little less. For me, her hatred was perhaps a two on a scale of five.

I had painted a better picture of myself due to my omnipresence in the ward, running around 24*7 for patients' preparation. Even when a patient was admitted in a different unit, I would listen to her, extract information on her disease, formulate a differential and start investigations. I needed to learn as fast as I could without wasting time. In the hospital, I would frequently bump into her while running around to finish the tasks at hand. She always smiled and enquired what I was up to. She occasionally stopped by the side of a patient's bed, while I was dressing the patient, peering into the scar. So, she saw me around often.

That day she walked into the OT and stood right next to us.

'So, you are doing the procedure today?' She looked at me expectantly.

'Yes ma'am.'

'Start, let me see.'

My senior froze. If we admitted that the scrubbing part was skipped, every one of us would be accused, starting from the consultant to the management of our college. There was always a regular, ongoing fight between government and private college managements, which we all wanted to avoid. It seemed as if we were being watched every minute. This government HOD, a spinster, had only one goal in life, and that was to hate us students and frown upon us. She hated that private management was handling the hospital, and resented that her role had been reduced to almost nothing. She roamed around aimlessly from ward to ward daily.

We knew that confessing our gross negligence would provoke a bunch of accusations, including blaming our management. We didn't want that eventual catastrophe. My senior nodded, and I held up the blade to cut, pausing for her to pass through to the other side of the OT. But she stood right there. I could feel her eyes on my gloved hands. I couldn't wait for long; I had to give the incision. One after another, I kept cutting the layers of the abdominal wall. Both me and

my senior were guilty of not sterilising the abdominal area. Nervously, with burdened heads, we moved forward with the last step of the surgery when she left us at last, satisfied with our surgical technique and skill.

I got a good scolding from my senior, followed by suggestions on how to prevent infection, suggestions on antibiotics to be given to cover gram positive, gram negative and anaerobic bacteria. We couldn't indent all these antibiotics, nor could we write on the file. We had to memorise them all, otherwise the nursing staff would question us. We had to somehow stop it from reaching the consultants.

'You are going to buy these antibiotics and it will be secretly given to the patient by you every eight hours, till she is in the hospital. Also, buy her medicines for another seven days for home. Make sure she comes to your OPD day for removal of her stitches,' I was instructed.

It was my first experience of performing a surgery; but instead of celebrating, I was sad, apologetic for my mistake and worried for the poor patient. The patient came to me after seven days; her wound was healthy. She was thanking me for all the personal care I took. I knew this had to be my first and last mistake of this kind.

MCD Hospital

IN THOSE idle days after returning from Mangalore, I first spent some much-needed time with my daughter, but alongside, I kept calling every government hospital in Delhi for a vacancy in OBGYN, SR (senior resident) post.

I never ever received any positive answer for three months. I began to think that I had frittered away my career and began to slip into depression and anxiety. I began suffering from lack of self-esteem and felt a loss of hope. Would I ever be able to become a good, skilful doctor?

One day, while sitting at my windowsill with my daughter next to me on one side, and with the telephone directory on the other, I dialed the next number in the series of MCD hospitals. The person on the other side answered the call.

'Hi, I am calling from Gurgaon, I was looking for a senior resident post in OBS and Gynae.'

The man replied, 'Are you from Gurgaon?'

'Yes, sir.'

'I am from Gurgaon too.'

'Ok, good, that makes us neighbours,' I chuckled, continuing the conversation.

'Do you have a car? How would you commute?'
'Yes, sir, I have a car.'
'That's good. Will you be able to give me a lift?'
'Yes, sir, sure.'
'That's good, take my personal number and meet me tomorrow in the hospital outside the MS's office.'
'Absolutely, sir.' I noted down his number.
'Doctor Sahib, you will pay me two months' salary in advance for allotting this seat to you. You must get ₹50,000 in a packet. Don't hand it over to me there. We will return home together by your car; I will take it from you then.'
I agreed reluctantly.
I couldn't sleep that night. I was going to be practising in MCD Hospital in Delhi, the busiest hospital there is. I was going to do surgeries all by myself. I was about to enter through the wrought iron gate into a world full of diseases, complications, emergencies, and emerge out, a winner.

IT WAS a different world. Patients from various socio-economic strata, diverse religious backgrounds and varying literacy classes were swarming with pot bellies, delivering year after year, for no reason or purpose.

The other day, all of us were waiting for rounds to start, loitering in the corridor, when one amongst us, an intelligent and driven doctor shouted at one of the pot-bellied patients who was trailed by four chirpy, bouncy children.

'Why can't you people understand, producing children is not the only work you are born to do!' She was visibly annoyed.

The mother of four was startled, but held herself steady

and fired her answer with the same pitch and intensity.

'We are not like you, unmarried till you are old and not able to produce like a female. You are barren, we are fertile, that's why you are jealous.'

Another day, while taking the medical history from one of the patients, I got frustrated. She was not able to reply to simple questions, like how many kids she has had, how many girls and boys, when her last period was, if her previous pregnancies were fine, etc. My job here was turning way more difficult than I had thought.

On another day, I found an old woman loitering close to me, and I proceeded to ask her what she was doing there.

'It's a labour ward, you shouldn't be here.' I noticed the toothless, grey-haired old lady with a big belly, looking at me hopefully.

'Are you pregnant? What's your age?' I couldn't suppress my curiosity.

'It's 30. I'm 30!' she said, shocking me out of my wits. She looked drained, her life, her youth squeezed out of her.

'How many children do you have?' I couldn't help asking.

'Eight', she answered nonchalantly.

'Look at yourself, lady. You look like a granny in your thirties. Why are you ruining your life, your body? Why can't you get yourself sterilised? How many more you want?'

She went silent. My desperation to teach her a lesson grew stronger.

'Until and unless you sign this sterilisation form, I won't let you inside,' I said firmly.

She didn't answer, and kept sitting quietly in the corner, taking every painful contraction silently. My order fell flat.

Her total silence made me angrier. I ignored her and turned to my routine of history taking, filling files, and shoving the herd to the examining room once again.

She looked at me every now and then, as if pleading to me through her eyes. She felt like pushing. 'Sign on the form and you are allowed inside,' I spoke. I was ready to take in the challenge.

'Doctor, in our religion, this is sin!' she protested meekly.

'Call your husband right now. You people have no other business than manufacturing kids every year. Government is providing free services to you, based on our taxes, and you are taking undue advantage of this. It is a serious issue,' the nurse said, backing me.

It didn't feel good to say this, but all of us were overworked and exhausted.

While this drama was happening, we kept on with our growing load of patients. The nurse was busy drawing blood for blood tests, cross-matching, labelling lab work. I was busy making entries into different registers and calling up the blood bank for bottles of one particular blood group.

Post-delivery excessive bleeding in already anaemic patients is a common phenomenon. Due to repeated stretching of the uterus in successive pregnancies, many a times the uterus doesn't contract immediately post-delivery. It can be fatal for the patient if the uterus will not contract to control bleeding blood vessels. A frail, torn uterus sometimes fails to regain strength and goes into atony. The vast, stretched uterine surface can drain as much as five litres of blood within minutes. This kind of postpartum death is common since ages.

Mumtaz Mahal while delivering her fourteenth child

with emperor Shah Jahan dying during childbirth was an apt reminder. Smita Patil, a film actor and recipient of Padma Shri Award too died of post-delivery complications.

Suddenly, one huge fist banged my table. I saw a tall broad, muscular, bearded man standing next to my chair, wearing a grave expression.

In a loud angry tone he enquired, 'Who asked her to sign on the sterilisation form?'

This was an unexpected attack which frightened me. I composed myself, collecting my courage.

'Sir, we thought she needed to know that such an option is available, if she wants it. We understand that it's your personal choice and it's fine if you don't feel okay about it,' I replied in a calm voice.

'No, I don't want it,' he replied flatly.

'That's fine sir. Please wait outside the labour room, we will take care of her.'

I allowed that lady in, took in a deep breath, trying to sweep away my morbid thoughts. The other doctors and nurses on duty witnessing this scene were laughing at me.

'What a pity! Our brave doctor buckled down, got scared of that man,' they remarked.

'Go and teach them the benefits of a small family, education, good health once again,' they said, mock sarcasm in their voices. To forget the incident, all of us ordered some tea and biscuits. The *chaiwala* was our favourite; he provided us life-saving drugs, blood and of course *chai* biscuit.

'Doctor Anu, please come fast, the LR3 patient is bleeding profusely,' a terrified voice shouted from inside. I searched in my purse, as the Prostodin injection was hidden

somewhere. Putting it into my lab coat pocket, I rushed to check Sushila's blood pressure, and the state of her postpartum womb. The uterus should have been contracted by now, where was it? I couldn't feel it under my hand, oh why couldn't I feel the contracted uterus?

She was going into atonic PPH (postpartum haemorrhage), and I feared her mental stress could cause her post-delivery bleeding, which could be fatal to her. Without wasting any time, with gloved hands I started massaging the uterus from abdomen and vagina, holding it tight between two hands and trying to squeeze it.

I used Methergine, a drug to contract the post-delivery uterus to stop the bleeding, patted the patient and enquired whether she was asthmatic.

'No,' the patient said.

'Let's give her Carboprost as well as an intramuscular stat,' I said.

This other drug, Carboprost was used to act on the uterine muscles to stop the bleeding from the expanded uterus.

Morning, eight o'clock, had always been a wrong time for any emergency to occur. The night staff is usually ready to leave by then, not interested in any new patient entering the labour ward, slowing the process of admission requisition and consent, resulting in slowing of the process of handover of duties to the morning staff. At the same time, the morning staff would enter lazily, fatigued after house chores, wanting to have some tea for relaxation before switching over to the hectic, tiresome duty ahead.

Therefore, that was a wrong time for any life-threatening emergency, as attendants were nowhere around, were not reachable even on the phone, and many announcements went unanswered.

Sushila, the patient was bleeding between my hands, and her newborn lying beside her was naked and crying at the top of her feeble voice. I was waiting for some help, but the nurses were still arguing about the change of staff, ignoring the pressing urgency. It was a crazy, overwhelming situation. Someone conveyed the news to the doctors' duty room, medical students from the hostel were summoned for blood donation, and another shot of injections was given to help the uterus contract. Our MBBS college students were aware of the drill; those kids were called in quite often to bleed for charity as attendants were either not willing or absconding to avoid donating blood for their own patient's life.

Once all the instruments were arranged, I retracted my hand from the patient's vagina, secured her urinary catheter, examined her perineum for any first or second-degree tear. However, thankfully no tear was found, confirming it as atonic postpartum bleeding. Her uterine cavity was explored to remove any placental membranes or retained placental bits which might be hampering the uterine muscles to contract.

Sushila was immensely patient; she let us do every procedure without moaning or crying in discomfort or pain. No anaesthesia was given during all the procedures—there was no time, we were busy saving her. But despite all the challenges, she cooperated with us silently, holding her baby tight near her. Her pulse was slow, her skin became cold, losing its colour, and her BP was falling.

'Where is blood, we need blood.' I was almost in tears by now.

The amount of blood lost had to be infused to save her organ system. Slowly, her kidneys would shut down without any blood supply and ultimately her brain—along with it, her lifelong agony would ebb away.

The intern got the blood, checked the crossmatch slip with the details in the file, a mandatory step to prevent wrong transfusion and started transfusion immediately from the second line. By now, her uterus felt a bit harder under my hand, and I nodded to relax everyone around. We sighed with relief. Soon, the uterus turned hard like a cricket ball inside the limp Sushila.

We celebrated our triumph with reassuring smiles as the uterus slowly began to control the bleeding by itself.

Everyone else quickly moved back to their respective wards, and their work went on, uninterrupted.

ANOTHER DAY dawned. It felt no different, till a shout shattered the routine.

'She killed her baby! Doctor, come quick!'

A lady in the bathroom had killed her newborn, throttled her to death. We were shocked. Everyone jumped on their toes and rushed towards the toilet.

This was nothing new. The ladies who had been delivering babies every year were way too experienced about all this delivery business. They very well knew 'that push' that got the baby out. They were audacious enough to check the gender of the new born just then. If it was a girl, they sometimes strangulated her then and there with their bare hands, right in front of the doctors, nurses or the *aayas*.

We peered inside the filthy toilet. Two *aayas* were trying to pull her out, the umbilical cord and placenta still attached to her womb and hanging from the vagina. The nurse separated the tiny, dead newborn girl from the cord.

The lady was stone-faced, with no visible regret or remorse on her face. She rather looked content after a war which had just ended, with destruction and pain all around. But she was still happy that she had saved herself. She was guilty of delivering a girl child, a grave sin, but she corrected it instantaneously. She fed her with her blood for nine months, she owned the life of that tiny being, so it was her right to take that away, she thought.

For some seconds, after the birth of the girl child, the mother could envision the cascade of events—an unwanted, unwelcomed child, abused, neglected, unloved throughout her life, transformed into a child-producing factory after being married off at a very young age. Yes, this was the horror story of her life.

After some conscious deliberation, she took a decision to deliver it secretly. If the newborn was a boy, she would shout for help, if it was a girl, she would kill her in the immediate moment and be relieved.

She was brought back to the ward, cleaned and covered. Her relatives were called to handover the dead daughter. No one mourned, no one came near the mother with empathy. I was quite sure that they were the driving force for her action.

I had to go back to the OPD. It was past ten, and I was already late. I rushed past many colleagues. Waving to everyone, greeting seniors, I noticed Dr Seema, smiling to herself outside the sonography room.

'Hey Seema, is there good news?'

'Yes!' She turned towards me, grinning from ear to ear.

'Congratulations,' I said, and passed by her hastily without waiting for an answer.

She has two daughters, and now she is pregnant again. She might be wanting a son this time, I assumed. She must have gone for gender confirmation too. But why am I thinking all this, I thought to myself while walking away. I tried to rebuke myself and flush these thoughts out of my mind. This boy and girl business seemed to cloud my mind as well.

The OPD was brimming with patients. How many of them were mothers who wanted to kill their daughters, and how many of them were mothers who were dying to have daughters, begging God for a chance to conceive?

If I were God, my earth would have been devoid of sorrow, I thought, as I sighed. The humans would get what they wanted; harmony and love would reign everywhere. If I were Him, I would empower all girls with education, self-respect, employment. I would empower every family with ideas about gender equality.

I turned to the woman who had approached me to talk about her disease.

'Rani,' I said, observing her file.

She leaned over me and said it was a very confidential matter and looked down at her feet.

'I am not able to have children,' she said, with a tinge of sadness.

'That's not a big issue, Rani. We get such cases and there are solutions,' I assured her.

'Doctor, I have been to every hospital, but there has been

no hope. Please give me a child, otherwise my in-laws will provoke my husband to remarry.'

She was sobbing now.

'Please hand over your previous reports and treatment details,' I said rather curtly.

She scooped out old, dusty papers and tattered slips from several government hospitals. Her dirty plastic bag was full of multiple test reports, lacerated X-ray films and numerous files. Searching through the pile, arranging them all neatly, year wise, I discovered her husband's semen report. It said Azoospermia.

'Rani, your husband has no sperm. However, you seem to be perfectly alright, all your test reports are normal, showing good fertility index and patent fallopian tubes. But the problem is with your husband, so stop running from pillar to post undergoing painful tests every few months.'

'Do you know that HSG (Hysterosalpingography) is a very painful test?' I asked.

'Yes, I am aware of it,' she replied quietly.

'And do you know that Azoospermia has no treatment other than borrowing donor (someone else's) sperms?' I asked again.

'Yes, I know that too!' she replied.

'In that case, did you undergo IUI (Intra Uterine Insemination) with donor sperm?'

'No doctor, my in-laws don't believe in that. They think it is sinful to even think of it! Trying to have a baby with another man's sperm is like adultery. I am helpless, doctor. The problem lies in him, still I am to be blamed for being barren.'

She started pleading now with her hands folded in prayer.

'Doctor, please do this IUI secretly. Once I am pregnant, all mouths will be shut. It's been fourteen years since my marriage and still I have not got acceptance from his family. I am living like a slave in that house, slogging from dawn till late night, doing every household chore, mopping, cleaning, cooking, washing clothes for all their family members. I am dependent on their mercy to get food and shelter for myself. My husband abuses me, he forces me to sleep with him and do unnatural acts of sex. I am living a life of humiliation every single day. Please doctor, arrange for this artificial insemination donor secretly for me. I will be indebted to you for life.'

I was shaken. Her plight seemed genuine. But still, helping her was illegal and hence, not possible. Without her husband's consent, impregnating her with donor sperm, was legally wrong.

I wanted to help her badly. Her vulnerability, her inability to conceive a child despite simple measures available to change her fate moved me. But my rational brain calculated the risks and I looked at her remorsefully.

'I am very sorry, Rani. I wish I could help you,' I said.

Impatient with my silence, she got up, collected her fate wrapped in ripped, soiled, fragile slips and went away from the OPD room.

Stop her, don't let her go. Whom will she go to? Where will I find her if I change my mind and think of doing something beyond the law, simply on the grounds of mercy? I heard a voice within me shouting at my ineptitude.

I headed to the canteen dejectedly. Dr Seema, my colleague, was also there at the table. I joined her for lunch, and out of

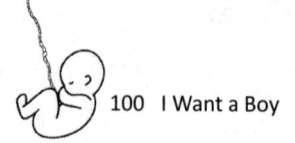

sheer curiosity, I enquired about her gestational age.

'Eight weeks as of now,' she said, and gently retired from the table. I guessed she had to rush back to work.

'Please excuse me, I am almost done with my lunch, I shall leave you to yourself, there is a lot of admission and discharge work to be done before four,' she said, hurriedly.

I smiled, knowing that she might be under tremendous work pressure. There were quite a few admissions: Three patients with pregnancy-induced hypertension, six for medical termination of pregnancy, three for permanent sterilisation and the others were antenatal admissions.

BY THE time I was done with work, I was longing to meet my daughter, who I knew, would be eagerly waiting for my tender, caring embrace. It was a pleasant surprise to see my parents playing with her. They gave a surprise visit to their granddaughter. What a relief, I thought.

However, we sensed some bitterness in the air. After a prolonged silence, my mother-in-law initiated the conversation.

'Your daughter thinks that we are not looking after her child properly. This is unnecessary stress in the family. Before it gets worse, please take your granddaughter with yourself, so that your daughter is at peace. I have not been in good health, but am still taking care of her child the whole day without any rest. But the situation has gotten worse with the passage of time, and I can't handle it anymore,' she said.

Everyone heard her attentively, but nobody could offer any solution to help her with her dilemma.

After the mess that I was in, while at home, I left for the hospital early the next day. It was quite a busy night, and the night doctors were struggling to keep up the pace.

With a total of about forty deliveries, including Caesarean and vaginal ones, and still many more awaiting their turn, it was an overwhelming scene. Patients were waiting either because no attendant was found to sign on the consent forms or crossmatched blood was not available in the blood bank or even worse, the donor (the attendant; husband or any other male member of the family) wasn't interested in donating blood for their labouring patients. It was a typical busy day for the Obstetrics ward.

Meanwhile, I heard the *aaya* shouting from the far end. 'Don't step on the filth, doctor, let me clean all the blood and trash. It's the mess you people create without thinking about us.'

I noticed the floor full of syringes, syringe caps, blood-soaked gauze floating in a pool of blood, a typical scene of post-delivery complications. We don't have bins, and sometimes they are broken, so they are of no use. I paused, but crossed it, nonetheless. There was a call from a fellow doctor working inside the LR.

The *aaya* was visibly annoyed. With a bang, she threw down the broom and left the LR, howling at the top of her voice.

'These young doctors do not respect us. It is becoming tough for us to work like this,' she sat in the corner sniffing her tobacco.

'I am not cleaning the filth created by you all.'

She must be sixty-plus, I thought. She had orange hair because of regular use of heena a well-built body, and exuding confidence that came from her permanent government job. No one could touch her position. We, the doctors on the other hand, were employed on an ad hoc basis or for a three-year tenure only. Her documents said that her age was forty-five, so she could be here for a good twenty more years, extracting regular pay cheques from the government till the age of eighty-five. I looked away, visibly upset by the negativity in the room. Thankfully, just then, Dr Seema called me in.

'There is another patient with ruptured uterus, previous Caesarean delivery, intra uterine death of the foetus. She was admitted as her labour was not progressing,' she explained to me.

'Why didn't you operate on her?' I asked out of curiosity.

'She has only arrived about ten minutes ago, dear.'

'Have we arranged the blood?'

'No, attendants said blood bank is currently full of blood units, that's why there is no need to donate.'

'But the blood units are to be replaced, didn't you tell them?'

'Any argument with them is futile, my dear.'

'But isn't it our responsibility to save every patient we can? We are doctors, after all, and will make every possible effort to cure them.'

Female attendants weren't allowing their husbands to donate blood, or else they would be weak.

'But blood is constantly regenerated in our bone marrow, and we can donate it after every three months. They don't accept it, don't want to understand it. To save a female, they can't risk a male's life. Such a pity,' I said.

'They are offering money to arrange blood.'

'Shall I arrange for buffalo or dog's blood? For a human to survive, we need another human. Moreover, it's only 100 ml blood, which the body replenishes within a month's time anyway!' I tried to explain to the attendant.

'Why don't you donate then?' she pounced upon me.

The neighbourhood ladies sitting in a circle seemed to have no better work but to talk against doctors.

'Don't give blood, they will arrange themselves. They always do. It's their duty.'

'My son is too weak to donate, or he is not in the country, or he is suffering from some illness.' They would make an excuse when approached.

If the son accidentally came forward, upon announcing his wife's name, the mother and her well-wishers would come to rescue him, assuming that as a government hospital, we always had all resources available, including human blood. We would go on explaining things to them, but it was useless, because it was their strategy to unnecessarily prolong the discussion. They seemed to have all the time and energy for *mohalla* gossip. They were precisely doing that today.

My head was aching. There was nothing to be achieved with such aimless conversations.

'If they don't agree to donate, whom shall I ask for blood?' I asked out loud, feeling anxious.

I noticed another patient with a ruptured fallopian tube, with terrible intra-abdominal bleeding. She had lost more than two litres of blood and was gasping. Her blood pressure was eighty systolic and she lay on the bed with feeble pulse rates and a pale face. What could we do as doctors to save such precious lives? Should we donate our blood in every shift to

save our own patients?

I was sinking with the weight of this paper in my hand, a paper on which Dr Seema had penned down the list of pending cases. All the patients were on the verge of dying. Something needed to be done to save them, within a few minutes.

My first job was to shift the ruptured fallopian tube patient for laparotomy.

'Let's stop the blood loss quickly,' I urged.

The anaesthetist was already in the OT. She had checked the consent form; the blood pints were in her hand, and she was pushing her trolley faster to the OT.

While checking her file, it was found that her tubectomy had been done about six years ago after she had given birth to two girls and a boy. Re-canalisation, the process of reopening her fallopian tube had been performed two years ago, after the death of her male child. Tuboplasty or reconstruction of fallopian tubes is a very delicate surgery. The possibility of a successful uterine pregnancy after such a surgery is as low as two per cent.

On the other hand, chances of tubal ectopic pregnancy are high. I am sure someone had explained it to her thoroughly, but she still risked her life for a male child. What if she died leaving her two daughters orphaned? But she didn't think about that, in her desperation to have a son.

In our country, the irrational wish to have a baby boy blinds everyone. People would adopt unrealistic methods to achieve the XY combination.

I assigned the case to Dr Rashmi and went to talk to another mob of attendants. There was another patient, bleeding profusely with low lying placenta. Her placenta—

the source of blood supply to the foetus was sticking low in the uterine cavity, resulting in the bleeding. The only way to deliver the baby was to perform a Caesarean delivery with an anticipation of immense loss of blood.

I started addressing the issue to a mob of men.

'See boys, I need four units of A-negative blood. Two units are available in our blood bank, other two will be arranged from the adjacent hospital. Four of you please come forward to donate the blood as soon as possible.'

They started murmuring among themselves in hushed voices, and after a while, an educated-looking man emerged to state a point on everyone's behalf.

'No one is willing to donate blood, but we can pay you in cash.'

The male relatives, friends and neighbours were standing beside the husband, providing no support whatsoever. They were just expressing their pity for the wailing husband, who might lose his wife and his unborn baby any minute to profuse uterine bleeding.

It was such a pity that her husband didn't feel like donating his own blood even after fifteen years of married life and having shared four kids with this lady. It was a myth prevalent among the masses that blood donation might weaken the man's libido or potency, and so the husband did not want to risk losing his orgasmic pleasure.

Nonetheless, the man took the blood sample and blood issue form from my hands to get the blood from other sources somehow, without donating.

We discussed alternative solutions, like plasma expanders till the bag of blood arrived, and started the surgery. She would

die if the bleeding uterus wasn't taken care of immediately.

On the other hand, there was yet another patient who was waiting with a 'dead foetus' inside her. Her uterus was torn from the previous Caesarean scar. Her urine got mixed with blood. Her abdomen showed two balls, one ball was her dead baby and another ball, her contracted, ruptured uterus. She was conscious, but too pale and exhausted to respond.

The samples were already sent, as the reports needed to be collected. I requested my intern to rush to the lab for test reports. In the hospital, we don't have a central system for moving blood samples, and for test reports. Class four workers are supposed to help with this task. The sample collection goes on throughout the day non-stop, so the reports need to be collected from the lab continuously.

Since the lab was situated at the far end of the hospital, it was an excruciating task, but then, that is how this job had been incorporated in our work list since years. The intern drew the blood, rushed to the lab to deliver the sample, came back, drew some more samples, returned to the lab, collected previously submitted reports and continued with the cycle.

On one hand, the *aayas* and other class four workers would take this opportunity to roam around the hospital, have their tea break, instead of coming back immediately. According to them, we, the doctors kept faking that the patients' condition is serious, or they needed emergency care, and worse that we were incapable of managing the emergency.

Bleeding emergencies, or dying patients are just normal everyday occurrences and they are in a constant argument that it is the young doctors' job to save them. They know that the young doctors are there for a three-year-tenure anyway, so they cannot care less for them. They even advise the attendants outside the labour room to not buckle down to the doctors' demand for blood. The *aayas* relate with that crowd more than they do with us, as they belong to the same socio-economic background. They believe our counselling on sterilisation, limiting the number of kids, and preaching about the importance of a girl child are plain nonsense.

On the other hand, we have also seen many smart young ward boys being a part of the blood bank racket. There's a booming business of organ or blood donation and the jobless young fellows are minuscule parts of it, demanding money for each bag of blood, arranging blood donors by unfair means.

After a while that day, the educated looking attendant arrived with four bottles of blood in his hand, and we rushed to the OT. I found the patient on the OT table, with the anaesthetist holding the oxygen mask on her face. Upon seeing me, he lost his calm, and started shouting.

'Doctor, you cannot leave a bleeding patient in the OT without blood or any gynae resident. I am stuck with this patient since an hour. My duty was over almost two hours back after the very busy night shift, but I am still stuck here, holding this oxygen mask without any gynae in sight,' he complained.

I was listening to him, matching the blood details written on the bag with that of the patient. I started passing the blood to her through one of her IV lines. There were tears rolling from the corner of her eyes, wetting the pillow. The anaesthetist left the operation theatre, saying he would send the morning duty anaesthetist. I was aghast, left helpless and alone with her.

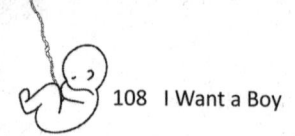

'Doctor, please save me. My children are alone at home, my younger son won't eat without me. He sleeps with me, and no one else. My children will be searching for me, please save me doctor,' she mumbled in a frail voice.

Five minutes of wait seemed too long, and the clock moved painfully slow. After a while, the day duty anaesthetist entered, released me from pumping oxygen to the patient and requested me to scrub. He started another IV line, and we checked if the blood was on flow. The patient was finally unconscious with wonder drugs. She was pain-free now.

We started the surgery. Her skin, muscle and sheath were cut, and as blood oozed out, her uterus turned blue. Her placenta was out first, followed by a huge retroplacental clot. We found the dead baby, his body smeared in thick, greenish amniotic fluid, and his own poop, which we call meconium. Her uterus was sutured after we tried to control the bleeding. Then the abdominal wall was sutured as well. The monitor showed her blood pressure.

Ninety systolic. Much better. I enquired from the anaesthetist if she was recovering. He nodded positively and smiled.

'She will come out of it, don't worry. She is a strong soul,' he assured me.

Though she needed three to four more units of blood to prevent DIC (Disseminated Intra Vascular Coagulation, a life-threatening blood clotting in every organ system) and oxygen support for few hours, I had a feeling he was right.

I felt guilty for expressing my anger on him when he had entered the OT. I was in panic with the Ambu bag in my hand, and rather surprised with the previous doctor who had left me in such a hurry. I might have said something to the morning shift doctor out of sheer annoyance. But without a word, he did his part patiently. He silently took on the responsibility and made me feel at ease so that I could go on with the surgery.

We need many such doctors with these qualities—the passion, sensitivity, and skill—that he was naturally endowed with, I thought. The beds are always full of ailing patients, the corridors crammed with patients awaiting surgeries or beds for treatment. There is a waiting list for beds, month after month. Every corner of the hospital is covered with sick humans swarming around. We need to either increase the capacity of our hospitals or slow down our birth rate. We need to stop all kinds of avoidable human infections (waterborne, mosquito-borne, or food-borne), we need to help those with easily treatable diseases, and we also need to save human kids with diseases due to malnutrition or infection which can really be prevented. We need to help them all—waiting for their turn in the OPD or OT. The more privileged ones get the preference, as they can bribe their way into the system.

The patient was wheeled out of the OT on a noisy, fractured, dented trolley, covered in a torn, blood-stained sheet. I patted her cheeks gently.

'Show your tongue, Rani,' I ordered.

She opened her moist eyes and reached out to touch my hand. We squeezed each other's hands, and a bond of kinship was formed in that moment. She was relieved to be alive. We smiled, as she closed her eyes with a peaceful grin.

'Everything is ok,' I said, and let her slide out of my sight towards the gynae ward.

Another patient with a ruptured uterus was awaiting surgery. I rushed down the staircase, from the fourth floor. There was no time to wait for the lift, just like we all did innumerable times of the day. In the foyer, I saw attendants, waiting for me to give them the news.

'She is out of danger currently,' I said, 'but would be needing a few more pints of blood.'

I informed them knowing quite well that it wouldn't be possible for them to arrange more blood. It was good that the lady was saved. Even if she were dead, her children would be the only sufferers. The husband would be the least affected. The children would have been motherless without a clue. Now that the mother was alive, they would be able to get her love and care and would be protected from worldly evil.

A sharp sting of happiness pierced my heart; a sweet pain choked my throat. This feeling of accomplishment after helping as many patients as possible, for hours on end kept me going. 'There should be zero maternal deaths'—this was the promise I had made to myself.

Collecting my scattered thoughts, I entered the LR. There was a shocking silence all around. I slowly moved towards the group of doctors surrounding the patient's bed. It was the same patient with uterine rupture, I discovered. What happened to her? Was she dead? She was fine with stable vitals when I had last seen her. My heart and brain were struggling to reason the inevitable. What if no senior doctor had come for rounds to check on her? What if Dr Rashmi was busy with other patients and was not able to monitor her vigilantly? But how could it be possible? Dr Rashmi is responsible; she must have done the needful; it must be something else.

I approached the head gynae, gathering my mental strength.

'Good morning, Ma'am!' I greeted in anticipation of a good scolding from my senior on rounds. According to her explanation, the patient might not have been managed well by me.

The patient looked quite familiar, and in good health. Where had I seen her, I wondered. Why was everyone around her if she was not medically serious? I also wondered about that.

'Dr Anu,' the senior consultant asked me, 'Don't you recall this patient? We did classical CS on her for her emergency.'

Yes, now I could connect to it all. On a very busy OPD day, this patient was brought to the hospital in a half-dead condition. Two elderly midwives and a few relatives were carrying her. Midwives had attempted normal vaginal delivery on her and failed miserably. The baby was lying in transverse position, hence vaginal delivery was impossible.

According to the midwife, they had delivered half the baby, but the other half was stuck inside. On further examination it was found that the baby's hand was hanging outside the vagina—limp, blue, listless. The head of the baby was on the right side of the womb and bum on the left side. The baby was lying in Buddha's posture inside the womb. Generally, the baby is in a vertical, head down position, for vaginal delivery to happen. In any other abnormal position of the baby, vaginal delivery is not possible, and shouldn't be attempted. In this case, the transversely lying baby couldn't be slipped out of the vagina.

Midwives kept pulling the baby's hand, and in the process, they could have dislocated its shoulder or elbow, inflicting grave injury to the baby, leading to its death. The mother's bladder and rectum was also crushed with the pressure of the dead foetus. It could have ruptured her uterus too, due to extreme stretching and thinning. The midwives must have tried every way to deliver the baby before bringing her to the hospital. They must have struggled a lot before finally surrendering to the obstetrician.

In this situation, the baby had also screwed a hole in the mother's urinary bladder, a condition called VVF, Vesico Vaginal Fistula. The continuous flow of urine through the vagina excoriated the mother's thighs, vulva, and the stench of urine was all over her body. Managing the issue of VVF had always been cumbersome for us doctors.

Eighty per cent of labouring women would deliver naturally without assistance. The number of labouring patients per day versus doctors and nurses are twenty to twenty-five per doctor at any given time in busy government hospitals. It is humanly impossible to attend or monitor every single patient on an everyday basis. They deliver naturally on their own. Sometimes we can catch the baby in time, sometimes it is born without any kind of intervention; at other times with the help of midwives.

The *dai* or midwife is usually self-trained. Without any formal training they carry out simple procedures, like giving IM injections, instilling vaginal labour-inducing gel etc. They have learnt the names and functions of many drugs and injections as well. They know which injection must be given to increase labour pains, stop post-delivery bleeding, enhance cervical dilation, and for labour analgesia. Now after many years of observation, they have also perfected the art of normal vaginal delivery. They have very powerful injections to hasten the delivery and for use in difficult cases.

The injections, which they refer to as 'magical potions', result in a positive outcome, when used on a labouring mother. Having no idea about the position of the baby in the womb, these *dais* often consider themselves better than doctors in this art. They believe we doctors do Caesarean deliveries unnecessarily, even when the presenting part is the head of the baby. All of them become normal delivery experts in their villages, till some catastrophe happens. Only then they bring those dying mothers to the hospital where they have worked for years as workers. In the hospital, they project themselves as respected delivery experts in front of a huge crowd, whereas in reality, they are the ones responsible for the deplorable condition of many patients. This happened to be one such case.

I noticed an intern running towards me. He shoved the patient's old file in my hands, the file with the details of her last Caesarean delivery, which was produced from the MRD section.

It read: 'Emergency CS done under spinal anaesthesia, *primi gravida* with transverse lie with hand prolapse (handled by a *Dai*).

'Abdomen opened, midline vertical incision, uterus opened through Kerr's incision, transverse. Amniotic fluid drained out completely, Meconium-stained baby tightly squeezed with uterine muscles. Incision on uterus extended to J shape in upper uterine segment to make space in tightly closed womb, baby delivered through Patwardhan manoeuvring, delivering shoulders first, followed by body, feet and finally the head.

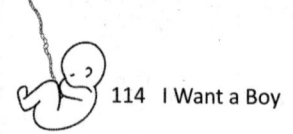

It is a very difficult method of delivery through Caesarean section. Morbidity to mother and foetus increases in this manipulation. Placenta and membranes smeared with thick MSL delivered, followed by closure of uterus and abdomen.'

A tiny human, having resisted death, was here, his blue body smeared in his own excretions, distressed without oxygen.

The baby must have indicated his distress during the delivery, but the *dais* would not have noticed. The foetal heart monitoring by stethoscope is not up to them. *Dais* at best can oversee spontaneous uncomplicated vaginal deliveries, with the babies popping out of the mothers' wombs every now and then in government hospital beds, but what about the complicated ones? In emergency delivery situations, they were never around. According to them, we must have woven false stories, manipulated the situation to do Caesarean deliveries to ease out our workload. However, that's far from the truth.

I could see that till the very last moment, the baby kept fighting. But the *Dai* never checked foetal heart rate, and she neither knew how to nor had the equipment. She did not realise every female body is different, and so is every delivery. No wonder there was such a huge burden on maternity units due to untrained *dais* and unmonitored home deliveries.

The senior consultant asked for the patient's discharge card. She was carrying it in a dirty bag with multiple other papers and lab reports. The discharge card was read aloud by the intern, suggesting that her next pregnancy should be booked in the hospital, and the delivery to be done by elective CS, as soon as she was thirty-six weeks in case she got pregnant again.

The instructions were explained to her clearly at the time of discharge. It was explained that timely LSCS should be done in next pregnancy, otherwise her uterus would rupture.

How could we make them understand the seriousness of a diagnosis?

It was so frustrating to deal with ignorance. I knew women like her would still follow the local *Dai*, even after such a disaster. They have always thought of us doctors as an anxious bunch of degree holders, scared of tiny medical situations. They have always believed that natural birthing is quite a simple thing, requiring no fancy degree or education.

'Dr Anu, shift this patient to the OT, take consent from her husband that hysterectomy might be required,' the senior consultant ordered me, frustration dripping from her voice.

'Foolish lady!' she said, annoyed, and moved to the next bed with a trail of junior doctors and nurses following her path.

The patient she was referring to was in front of me, a twenty-four-year-old woman. Previously, she had given birth to a dead baby due to obstruction in labour delivered via C-section. The second time, her pregnancy was terminated due to uterine rupture, again due to an unnecessary trial of labour on her already scarred uterus, while she was clearly advised to come for an elective C-Section at thirty-six weeks of her gestation.

We saw her husband standing in a corner, reluctant to sign on the consent papers for her hysterectomy. His mother was there with him, with her fake cries.

'These hospitals are open only to sterilise our daughters and daughters-in-law. It was wrong on our part to bring

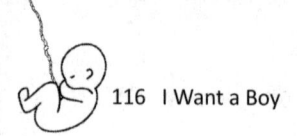

her here, they say they will operate to deliver the baby but instead, they are removing the uterus. I have delivered seven children at home without any difficulty. I never saw the face of any hospital. I told you to not come to the hospital, the doctors here have no knowledge of vaginal delivery. They are here to operate upon us just to earn money,' she wailed and complained.

'Oh, my God, I will die without seeing my grandson's face! God will never allow me to enter the gates of heaven. Without a grandson, our family legacy will end! This girl has ruined my son's life. Since the day she has come, not a single day has been joyful. How we are wasting our money on her operations one after another! This money would have been used for your business,' she wailed, her complaints continuing along with her shrill cries.

'No one from her maternal family has shown up yet, as if she is only our responsibility. We are so miserable,' the lady kept on wailing, cursing the pregnant girl with a dead foetus and ruptured uterus, following an exhausting twenty-four-hour labour.

For no fault of hers, the girl was lying, half-unconscious and frail on the OT table, waiting to be saved by removing her uterus. Married at the age of nineteen, she got pregnant twice in succession—carrying her pregnancies for nine months. The first pregnancy ended in obstructed vaginal delivery with the death of her unborn child, the second one ended in uterine rupture. Losing two babies in a row, she would now lose her womb at the age of twenty-four, losing her ability to conceive in the future.

She was an uneducated young soul, earlier dependent on

her father and later, on her in-law's family. Neither she, nor her illiterate husband were aware of medical facilities offered to them in government hospitals—free of cost, along with antenatal visits, vaccinations, and supervised deliveries. Her mother-in-law was illiterate too, with no faith in the medical system. Home deliveries by the *Dai* was the norm in their culture, which explained why she didn't allow the young girl to visit the hospital for antenatal purposes.

Moreover, she was blaming her for not being able to deliver vaginally. Why couldn't she deliver her baby normally when her mother or mother-in-law had home deliveries? Her abnormal womb was under merciless scrutiny.

The senior consultant sutured her uterus layer by layer, reshaping the womb, reconstructing her fertility. Without her womb, she would be thrown out. Her husband would remarry for a progeny. She would either be sent back to her parents or live a life of humiliation as the childless first wife living with his family, only for food and shelter. It was important to give her fertility back to her. I was amazed with the marvellous result. My senior performed a fine surgery. I was filled with gratitude towards her. I wondered why I felt this kinship within me for every patient I treated.

Our team of doctors delivered a dead male baby of 3.2 kilogram from the abdominal cavity, washed all the blood and blood clots thoroughly before closing the abdominal wall. It was heart breaking to see a dead baby who was healthy before the delivery. The only solace was that the mother could be saved with her womb still inside her.

With relief, I informed her husband that she is good and will be able to conceive, but they must try to delay her

conception for at least two years.

'Please book her for an antenatal check-up on a regular basis,' I told him.

The most important reminder was not to try vaginal delivery and home birthing, strictly C-section at thirty-six weeks. I even shared my personal phone number with him so that he could be in touch once she conceived, though I knew I would be somewhere else after two years. Still, I wanted him to understand the severity of the situation and get help for his vulnerable wife.

It was two o'clock. My stomach was making gurgling sounds. But my labour room rounds were still pending. I decided to leave it to a junior doctor. What if another complicated case awaited? Hastily, I stepped downstairs to the labour room.

The junior doctor was handling six labour tables single-handedly. Two others were busy managing the OPD in flow.

'Hey girls, have you had your lunch?' I asked the others in the room.

'No!' the voices echoed in unison.

'Ok then, start going one by one. Let me handle the OPD patients. Return fast. Don't take more than fifteen minutes, and on your way please ask *dhabawala* to send six cups of tea to LR.'

I finished the queue of patients at hand quickly, to help the junior doctor struggling alone with six labouring tables, delivering babies, and transferring patients to and fro. It was the duty of the senior doctor in charge to make sure that everybody had their meal on time, and also that the labour room functioned smoothly no matter what.

At the end of the usual rigmarole of the delivery room, when the batch of junior doctors came for duty, we rejuvenated ourselves with tea from the nearby *dhaba*. The wards were full with each bed being occupied by two patients. From the first to the last bed, it took close to one hour thirty minutes to take rounds, put orders and execute drug delivery. By the time examination and files were complete, a few of them started pushing the baby out and we were shifting them to labour tables one after another.

I sent the last junior doctor to have lunch by 3.30 pm and straightened myself up to catch half a dozen deliveries before my shift got over at 4 pm. By this time the previous batch of junior doctors had come back.

Soon the clock struck four and our saviours, the doctors of the next shift, were here to take over.

We took a deep sigh of relief while hugging the shift doctors. 'It's your turn, soldier, hold the front,' I said, and walked out of the labour room.

Scattered thoughts and images started playing in my brain's reel. Placenta previa, ruptured uterus, *Dai* handled MTP and so on. Was it possible to change this sick society? My car started moving, the stories I lived during the day floated over my head, and like a zombie, I drove towards home.

My little innocent child was waiting for me at home. Perhaps there was a biological clock set in her body. She could sense that I was late by a few minutes by the time I finally returned home. Every minute passed in anticipation of my return. And what a wonderful sight it was to look at her face light up with happiness and excitement, seeing me entering that door.

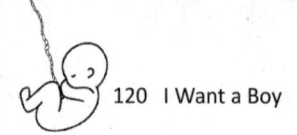

I lifted my angel up and placed her on my lap, kissed her several times, hugged her small, soft, chubby body. This, to me, was the most satisfying, loving moment; her giggles, sounding like melodious music, the spark in her eyes, appearing bright as moonshine. My daughter, my love. I made my way into my room after playing with her and tucking her into bed. The nights were filled with dreams of labour room patients.

'HEY SUNDARI, look at your baby!' the doctor was shouting at her. The newborn baby girl was hanging upside down, the obstetrician grabbing her tiny feet with her hands.

'What is it? A boy or a girl, asked the doctor. But the patient wouldn't answer. She glanced at her daughter and looked away. She didn't seem to want her or acknowledge her presence. She kept mum.

The doctor yelled at her again, 'Sundari, please speak and confirm whether it's a girl or boy.'

The baby was still hanging in the doctor's right hand, getting rubbed gently with her left hand so that she could cry and breathe. The umbilical cord was still attached to the mother's placenta. But the patient was blankly staring at the cracked, blood-stained wall of the labour room. The doctor couldn't cut the cord till she confirmed the sex, and the delay could be mortal to the baby due to the overload of blood from the placenta.

The doctor on duty was tired and exhausted after the night duty. The labour room was busy and noisy. Screams and groans of labouring patients echoed in the room, overwhelming her fatigued brain. The wards were packed with double capacity.

Each bed was occupied by two labouring women, lying on cracked, sodden mattresses in each other's blood and amniotic fluid. Ragged bed covers and torn sheets were shielding few of them. There was no screen between the beds, with which some kind of privacy could be maintained. It was like a big hall with twenty beds and forty or more patients, crying in labour with leaking or bleeding vaginas, trying to find a place and position.

The provision of hiding behind covers could not be afforded. The front wall was a glass window partition, looking towards the hospital entrance. The huge glass window was covered by tattered curtains, and newspapers were pasted with tape. The labour room was in a truly poor state, providing a voyeuristic view to anyone entering the hospital. The frustrated doctor called out to the nurse. After multiple shouts from the ward, a nurse strolled in with an annoyed expression.

'What is it doctor, why are you shouting? There is a hell of a lot of work pending. What is it?'

'Sister, the lady is not uttering the sex of the newborn. I can't cut the cord. The baby will die of cold and overload. Please do something.'

Nurses in government hospitals are not to be ordered. They are permanent employees. Nurses have seen many such doctors come and go. They handle the erratic and unreasonable behaviour of their patients. This is just a routine job for them, which they perform as reflex action. They would just ignore the junior doctors' commands when told to perform such trivial duties.

Without noticing or ignoring sister's irritation, the doctor requested her to persuade the patient to announce the sex of the baby before cutting the cord. Generally, the nurses are very good at it, since they admonish the patients and convince them to speak up. But this time, she was disturbed and annoyed at the call for such an idiotic job, and she did something terrible; she moved towards the patient and slapped her hard, hurling abusive words at her in quick succession.

'What insane behaviour!' I said, shocked and astonished. But the nurse was unfazed, and another slap followed.

The stubbornness reached its peak when the patient didn't cry or moan and kept lying there expressionless as a stone. The mother of the newborn wouldn't announce that she had delivered a daughter again. A fresh gush of blood poured from the vagina into the perineal bucket on the floor. The mother's placenta was separating.

A cat was perched on the windowsill, waiting in anticipation of devouring the placenta. The cat was at home here in the hospital and was a permanent resident of the labour room ever since she was a kitten. The feline knew that she would be able to feast on the placenta as soon as it was dropped into the perineal bucket.

Our rather ferocious furry friend also knew that no one in the room would ever try to stop her from getting her bloody meaty meal. The rest of the team were busy with the baby's delivery and would usually be gathered around the mother when this happened.

The officials were in complete apathy about cats and dogs roaming around within the hospital premises and everyone pretended that they just did not exist.

I was also too busy to bother about the cat.

'Sister, please add ten units oxytocin to the drip,' I ordered.

Sister gazed at me, conveying her disapproval.

'Doctor, please ask your juniors to do all this. Let me go and call her attendants before the placenta comes out. Once placenta is out, we won't have any proof that the girl belongs to her.'

The nurse rushed and called out for the relatives of Sundari to come near the labour room gate. The big veranda in front of the labour room was full of people. Aged grannies, mothers and mothers-in-law, sons and brothers, kids of every shape and size filled the space. Morning tea was getting distributed with rusks and biscuits. People were spread on bed sheets, *dari, chattai,* chatting in between their sips of tea. The labour room brought good news of new babies being born, congratulations echoed, followed by distribution of sweets.

'Relatives of Sundari, please come to the labour room gate.'

The announcement echoed in the veranda, startling the mother-in-law of Sundari. She prodded her daughter to listen to what the nurse had to say. The lady rose from her resting position and motioned towards the nurse.

'Come on, quick, it's an emergency!' the nurse pulled the sister-in-law inside.

Pointing towards one of the labour rooms, she pushed the lady inside and asked her to tell the sex of the newborn hanging upside down in the doctor's hand. The newborn's brain was flushed with blood.

Pulling her veil on her mouth, the sister-in-law examined the sex of the baby closely and declared bitterly, leering at the mother, 'It's a girl!'

'Good,' replied the nurse. 'Now get out from here, and

let us do our work. Already too much time has been wasted because of this dumb lady.'

The doctor cut the cord, and delivered the placenta, even as our fat cat was waiting to grab it from the bucket. Meanwhile, the newborn was handed over to the nurse to be examined by the paediatrician.

A couple of injections to contract the uterus were given prophylactically to prevent postpartum bleeding. I started suturing the perineal cut without local anaesthesia, as I knew requesting the nurse for it would trigger off her unnecessary wrath. And no one else was around to fetch the anaesthetic drug or even the syringe. Episiotomy suturing was needed urgently to stop bleeding. Sundari lay motionless, tears coursing down her cheeks, struggling with the unexpected result of her fifth pregnancy and childbirth. She knew a bitter, cruel reality waited for her outside the labour room.

Her devious sister-in-law embraced her mother, feigning a grief-stricken expression. 'It's a girl again!' she said, almost crying.

The elder daughter-in-law sitting next to her mother-in-law was now relieved of her dominance. Her undisputed position as a mother of a son, mother of the heir to the family was retained. She had achieved it through fifteen years of resilience, humiliation, and torment after finally delivering one son after four daughters.

Sundari's mother-in-law started crying out loudly. 'She must not have taken the holy drug rightly. Her evil spirit will ruin my son.' Everyone was watching the tragedy, listening to her wails, sympathising with Sundari's family.

'I want a Boy...' Aarifa's Story

IN THE ward, I happened to work with this beautiful nursing staff, Aarifa, a girl with creamy rosy cheeks and dark black hair tied in a ponytail. She smiled gently while sliding from one bed to another, tending to her patients. Even after two LSCS (Lower Segment Caesarean section), she looked like a young girl, a true Arabian beauty. I became fond of her. She talked smoothly, patiently, with an inner sense of calm. At the age of twenty-six she appeared matured and composed. We used to chat about patients and treatment options, and about other hospital stuff, very rarely about her daughters. Both of us were mothers, and like me, her life too, revolved around them. I admired her for her beauty and her maturity.

With our rotation duties, from one ward to another after every three months, we missed meeting each other for more than six months. On returning to the same ward as hers, I found she was absent. After a couple of days, my curiosity grew. I knew she wouldn't leave a permanent pensionable job. She had bought a small house and was paying mortgage. I asked one of her colleagues if she was on leave.

'Aarifa is no more, doctor,' a fellow nurse replied.

Unbelievable. It can't be true. It shouldn't be true. The whole world whirled in front of my eyes. What would happen to her daughters? How did this happen? She was fit, perfectly healthy. I wanted to shout, cry out loud. It was a jolt, a shock that numbed my senses.

The sister replied, 'Doctor, she was our batchmate in nursing school, in the same hospital, the only child of her parents. She was a Sikh, very delicate and beautiful.'

What? Was she not a Muslim? I always looked at her as a Persian beauty.

She died during her third Caesarean delivery. It was a case of placenta previa. Doctors had advised her sterilisation as a third pregnancy seemed likely to turn into placenta accreta (blood vessels piercing the wall of the womb to enter the urinary bladder). It was a dangerous condition where she could have bled to death. And I suppose that was what happened in the end.

'She herself was a nurse, why did she go for a third pregnancy?' I couldn't help asking.

'Her husband wanted a baby boy.' It was a statement which leaves no place for any logic or argument. A beautiful, financially independent wife was not enough.

The nurse continued, 'It was her bad luck, doctor. During our nursing training, this boy was a regular visitor in this hospital, bringing his sister, sister-in-law, or neighbours for gynae-related issues. He fell for her beauty, and started following her, gifting her flowers, suits, or jewellery. We warned her many a times. He was uneducated, living with a dozen of his family members in a dingy old haveli in Darya Ganj. He

was helping his brother in a small-time shop in Sadar Bazar. No degree, no regular income, no home, dependent on his family. But she was madly in love. Her parents tried talking sense to her, but it was all in vain.'

Despite her beauty, job, education and dowry, she was not accepted in that Muslim family. She converted her religion, changed her name, but was still hated by her sisters-in-law for she was better than them in all respects. Her daughters were taunted as 'angrez' for their education in an English school. She braved all odds, separated from her parents, all for his sake. Her parents kept on supporting her, through their son-in-law. This fellow knew that her parents would do anything for their daughter's happiness. He demanded money, a bike and so on from them from time to time. She was not aware of all this for a long time. She delivered two daughters in succession, joined the hospital, and got a copper-T inserted for contraception. She was not her chirpy self. She kept herself busy, and never spoke much. I think she repented her decision, but she knew she couldn't reverse it, so she tried to live with her destiny with bravery and fortitude.

It was easy for the women of the house to gang up together and turn the good-for-nothing husband against his own wife and daughters. Even in her second delivery, five units of blood were transfused. Her uterus was badly torn with a completely removed placenta previa. She had to stay in the hospital for four weeks. Her husband came after a week to mourn the second daughter's birth. She was broken physically and emotionally.

To keep the marriage going, and not giving anyone a chance to humiliate her parents for her bad decision, she kept on carrying this burden on her shoulders. She was accused of wasting money on her daughter's education in an English-medium school. To get out of the toxic environment, she applied for a house in a housing society, and took a loan which would be cleared in a few months. She wanted to give better surroundings to her daughters and take them away from the toxic, orthodoxy at her husband's home. She was very excited to get the possession of that flat.

Now her husband will get to keep the house. He has already pulled out his daughters from the school. Aarifa should have thought about her daughters. She was bleeding from her third month onwards. She refused to consult us out of shame. She didn't get her antenatal booking, no tests, no vaccination, nothing this time. Her family took her to a small-time nursing home without blood bank or ICU facility. A son was delivered, leaving her bleeding to death.

Now the husband is married again, with a son, two daughters, a house, and her PPF money. He is not willing to hand over Aarifa's daughters to her parents for better care. Her parents are living in sheer hell, crying for their daughter and grandchildren.

I couldn't bear hearing the rest of the story. I walked away, hiding my tears.

Being doctors, we prepare ourselves daily to deal with patients who undergo post-delivery bleeding complications. The uterus can bleed like a waterfall and litres of blood can gush from the vagina within minutes. It's a scary sight. At such times, no amount of uterine massage, or uterotonic drugs help. The patient bleeds drop by drop, till every molecule of her blood is drained into the bin, on the floor, in front of the doctors. We see a life being born and another being taken away from this world. We see a mother conscious of her departure, leaving her child at the mercy of her relatives, and it pains us no end.

I was living each story, each life. But life moves on. Many Aarifas are dying still, in the maternity wards, leaving motherless children behind, leaving their mourning parents, leaving a careless, happy husband with all the wealth she left for him. When I was with them in the hospital, they were part of my own kith and kin. As soon as I would be back home, these stories would be stored safely in one of the brain's compartments. I cursed myself silently every day. Was I doing anything for Aarifa's daughters, or her parents or for many other motherless children?

Maternal deaths have been so common in our country, due to anaemia, pregnancy induced hypertension, *dai*-handled deliveries, multiple successive births, illegal, unsafe abortions and many more reasons. Many of these deaths are preventable and the deaths that do occur because of these reasons can be termed 'criminal'. A child's birth is a miraculous, divine phenomenon and should not carry the blemish of a maternal death.

My Abortion

I WAS falling with my eyes facing the brim of the well, slowly, gradually, sinking, as light as a feather. I was under a strong delirium; my brain was not working. I was awake and aware, but not afraid. I could see long hollow holes in the boundary wall of the well all around me. The spaces were occupied with dead bodies of women, covered with a slimy, mucinous, transparent, and slippery substance. I could see familiar, expressionless faces in the water. I think they were dead. Under the effect of the anaesthetic drug, Ketamine, the patient loses touch with reality.

'Hold her tight, else her body will fall,' I heard a voice say.

'Two of you, hold the legs, you come for the back, and I will hold the head…. One, two, three….'

My body was being shifted from one place to the other by four people. I could not feel any connection with my body. They were probably taking my body somewhere and suddenly bodies smeared with slime started sliding, cascading over me, submerging me under them.

Why am I not revolting, I thought, in shock. These sticky

bodies will pile up over me, asphyxiate me, kill me.

Where are my nerves, my spinal cord? I was dying, yes, I was dying, now my thoughts would stop once and for all.

'Show your tongue,' somebody tapped my cheek.

'Try to open your eyes.'

'What's her name, doctor?' somebody else asked.

'Dr Anu, Hello, Dr Anu, the procedure is done.'

'I hope you didn't feel any pain.'

'Hope you are alright and fit to have some sips of water after three hours.'

'Please show your tongue.'

With great difficulty and labour, I pulled my tongue out.

'I will take your leave, Dr Nathani,' the anaesthetist said.

'Yes, please come to my chambers for your payment,' Dr Nathani requested the anaesthetist.

I recollected my memories; I had come to this nursing home for medical termination of pregnancy some two hours back.

Disturbed and crying, I entered into the doctor's chamber. I apologised and requested her to perform termination of my foetus. I couldn't look into her eyes. I felt ashamed of myself. Remorsefully, I signed the consent form and gave it to my husband to sign. I could not stand against this heinous decision despite being a doctor myself. How long were they going to punish me and abort my baby girls?

It was painful, harmful to the body, draining me mentally and physically. In that moment, I hated myself, my partner, and his parents. I hated patients who would commit female foeticide. I hated the world.

I lectured them on the importance of daughters and their

human rights. I maintained that nobody could force them to undergo such a procedure. You are educated, stand up for yourself, for your self-esteem, I would say to them, time and again. But they would hear it and leave in search of another clinic with the desire of getting rid of their unwanted daughter. I was recently married then, and doing my internship.

After seeing the way my patients were humiliated for delivering a girl child, post-delivery, I could understand the burden of being a daughter's mother. A huge burden of hatred towards my patients evaporated; instead, a feeling of compassion and pity filled my heart. I ached for them and pitied myself.

The female population is decreasing in every passing census, which is a really disturbing news. It upsets me because I am a girl, and more so because I am a mother to a girl. And above all, I am not able to conceive a baby boy. Can't there be equal distribution of daughters and sons by the heavens? Why did my sister deliver one son and the second time, twin boys, when she was desperate for a daughter?

Why was it not God's duty to make fair distributions? It, therefore, seemed fair on my mother-in-law's part to keep asking me to abort every girl child till I conceived a boy—so much so that I wanted to take my own life after giving them their much-awaited heir.

My conscience was eating me alive, every three months following the brutal termination of my tiny girl foetuses. However, I kept on getting it done, hoping to kill myself in the process eventually. My tormentors were more important to me than my own offspring, an innocent child who needed me through her childhood and adolescence.

Why was I ignoring my daughter, being so heartless? I needed to live for her. Why was I on the path of self-destruction? I was suicidal, inflicting repeated abortions, hoping to die on the delivery bed.

Today I can feel the pain of every single female in want of a male child. I tried to counsel and guide them, but to no avail. I understand them now; they were determined to commit this heinous crime, because they thought it would change their destiny, improve their lives and their already troubled relationship with their in-laws. Every strong and fit creature wants to win the battle of life. The poor, the naive and the weak do not have a right to live.

DR ASHA'S OPD was always busy, with an average of close to hundred patients every day. She was in her seventies. Dr Asha with her fair skin, hunched back, red lipstick, red nail paint, and beautiful floral printed saree, was quite a force to reckon with. With her resident doctors, her behaviour was very difficult and unpredictable. Her husband, Dr Saxena also worked in the same hospital as a paediatrician, but he did not have a thriving practice.

Dr Saxena didn't believe in entertaining patients as she did. Even if she tried to deliver all her patients on his call day, the patient would cancel their follow up visits with him due to his disinterest in answering questions or explaining important things. They were looking for answers on how to swaddle the baby, which oil was best for massage, why their baby was not growing in inches every week, and they wanted a more patient, competent doctor for these queries, which Dr

Saxena was not. Therefore, despite delivering all the patients by Caesarean section on her husband's call day, Dr Asha could not boost her husband's paediatrics practice.

In the OPD room, one resident sat with her, writing prescriptions as she dictated, while another resident stood, trying to help the patient lie down on the bed. She would welcome the patient with her friendliest grin and compliment her for her beauty or attire. Then with softness in her tone, she would ask the patient her complaints. Her expression would grow serious upon listening to the tiniest of the patient's problems. She would then order the resident to help the patient, while explaining the severity of her UTI or vaginal infection to her spouse or mother-in-law or whoever had accompanied the patient.

A customary look at her perineum behind the curtains followed by a pap smear done by the resident doctor usually completed the examination. If there were some tests reports produced, it was the sitting resident's duty to summarise these for her. She would prescribe two to three antibacterial and anti-fungal medicines to every patient. The treatment was almost always the same cocktail therapy to cover every bacterium and fungus. She didn't believe in tailor-made or evidence-based management, but in a multi-drug approach, which was unethical and wrong, but as resident doctors, we were mute spectators.

As for her patients, they were happy to be consulting an experienced and famous gynaecologist who had delivered their moms or other relatives in her long practice of fifty years. They believed every word she said.

It was an unsaid rule that each one of her full-term patients would get admitted for induction of labour on Wednesday evening and deliver by Thursday night by vaginal or caesarean section, just because that was Dr Saxena's call day as the paediatrician. There was absolutely no spillover on Friday or no early delivery on Wednesday by natural progression or emergency surgery. She would get really upset if delivery of even a single patient happened on another paediatrician's call day.

I remember how her long, bony fingers would shake while trying to deliver the baby. We supported her hands standing beside her, knowing that she might drop the baby. Even during caesarean deliveries, we would be soldiering every move of hers, knowing that her shaky movements might give a ragged cut somewhere or the other. We were alert at every step to anticipate the next wrong move and correct her instantaneously. Still, every time, without fail, she took all the credit for delivering the babies.

However, the reason of her popularity was known only to her pet residents, mostly because she preferred only that one resident in her OPD on daily duty as well as on Thursdays. All others were kept out of this secret formula of how to exponentially grow your practice.

One day, while I was on duty, a beautiful tall, fair *sardarni*, with pink lipstick, mascara, and oodles of makeup got admitted with labour pains. It was her third pregnancy, though she looked like a new bride in her embroidered salwar suit. She was smiling with every painful contraction, and I liked her positivity as well as her flawless beauty.

We chatted during her labour, about her rich background, their family business, and about her two young daughters. It was a quick, easy delivery as the baby passed through her wide, lax birth canal. However, we discovered after her labour that her beautiful exterior hid her weak abdomen and perineal muscles. She hadn't done any exercises to strengthen her perineum or abdomen in between her earlier pregnancies which had happened in quick succession, year after year. Throughout her labour, she had smiled and laughed with every bout of pain. I was amazed at her tolerance threshold and perseverance, as if she knew the outcome was going to be different this time.

Yes, she delivered a baby boy, and she was confident of this fact, even before her delivery.

That's when she revealed the secret of her happiness during one of her painful contractions. She confessed that she had gone through selective sperm insemination for having a baby boy. She also let us know how Dr Saxena had saved her life and put a stop to the repeated abortions she had undergone to kill her female foetuses. I was listening attentively to every word she was saying.

It suddenly occurred to me to take the number and address of that centre, where this selective IUI was being done. I told myself it might come in useful. One the one hand, I was disgusted listening to the wrong practice followed by my reputed senior, but on the other, I reasoned that demand generated supply.

From then onwards, I started tracking patients who had visited for injections post-IUI. I enquired about their kids' gender, and about their reason for IUI. Dr Saxena was secretly blessing the couples with sons through a series of instructions, including a strict-diet formula, sex postures, fertile days of cycle for baby boy, medicines to improve vaginal health to attract male sperms and improve quality of eggs before taking the final step—selective insemination of male sperms into their wombs by artificial insemination. It was successful in more than eighty per cent of the cases.

Many years later, after my own repeated female abortions, I recollected the day when I had met the sardarni. It was she who had spoken highly about Dr Saxena and Dr Krishnan. The latter doctor had given her a positive result—a baby boy.

I turned to my small diary with its golden cover. It was right there, the address and landline number of Dr Krishnan in South Delhi. I was sick of the multiple abortions I'd been put through, and it had begun feeling like it was a never-ending process. The more I thought about visiting the doctor, the more it seemed logical. Instead of killing a child in the womb, why not aim for the desired gender and be done with it?

I located the lab; it was somewhere in a residential area far away from the main market. We climbed up the narrow staircase to reach the first floor. Right there at the end of the staircase, we almost hit the glass door that read 'Dr Krishnan's Lab' in big letters. The interiors were impressive, neat, and warm. A lady at the reception greeted us and asked for my doctor's prescription.

'Dr Saxena has sent me to Dr Krishnan,' I replied, quite instinctively at that moment.

'Yes ma'am, I understand, still I need a prescription to know what needs to be done.'

'Oh ok, I am a doctor myself,' I replied.

'Can I meet, sir, personally?'

With hesitation, she requested for my ID. I had left that job long back. I didn't have any proof of my identity. And I

didn't even have my business card because I was not practising anywhere at the moment.

'My husband has his ID, will that do?' I asked.

She took his ID, xeroxed it, gave it back to us and headed to the doctor's chambers.

Within a minute, he called us in and stood up to welcome us. He was a very warm and handsome doctor. I felt guilty coming here with such an insensitive question on my mind. He greeted us and enquired what it was that had made us visit him. I felt very heavy inside, and my throat went dry. I was not able to swallow, nor was I able to speak. How could I tell him what I needed without sounding like a horrible person? But then again, that sardarni and many other patients had done this. Did he do selective sex IUI?

How was I going to ask him though? What if he got offended, or what if he judged me? I was struggling within.

He was patient, composed, and was waiting for me to speak.

I mumbled, 'Sir, we want a baby boy.'

'Ok,' he said.

'Ok, very well,' he said, and took out a prescription pad from his drawer and prescribed some medicines for my husband and asked us to come for an ultrasound on the twelfth day of my cycle. 'We will do what we can to help you have a baby,' he stated and showed us out.

For the next three to four cycles, I followed the same routine. I got an ultrasound every alternate day from the twelfth day, and then called my husband on the day of ovulation for artificial insemination after preparation of semen. Sperms carrying female chromosomes were discarded by chemical processing. Only those sperms carrying Y chromosomes were inserted in my uterus.

In my third attempt after three months of regular IUI cycles, the pregnancy test showed two pink lines. We were happy for a successful outcome, and hoped it was a male foetus. But the happiness didn't last long. I aborted spontaneously around six weeks. There was no cardiac activity in the foetus.

WE STARTED a new job in a far-off village in Haryana, struggling with our duty roster and regular visits to this clinic, commuting 90 kms every time, for the positive outcome. But every time, the pregnancy wouldn't proceed past eight weeks. Twice, I got suction evacuation done. In the fourth attempt, it did grow close to twelve weeks, but on the day of sex determination by ultrasound, it was once again, female despite IUI. We were among the twenty per cent failure cases. And I underwent an abortion again.

I was losing faith and my self-respect. As it is, I had lost faith in the sanctity of marriage in which people went against God's wishes and selectively wanted to give birth only to a boy child. This obsession by my husband's family for a boy had turned even me into a monster, a murderer. I hated myself, and my existence. I didn't go back after that abortion. After a few months of fighting, arguments, and emotional drama for the heir of the family, I gathered my courage again and entered the battle to deliver a boy by any means.

I finally conceived a boy, but after 12 weeks, I started bleeding owing to repeated abortions, low lying placenta and so on. I stopped my practice which was in its starting phase,

and went on to complete bed rest till the eighth month.

I finally delivered a baby boy–a child whom my husband and my in-laws had been waiting for all these years.

His birth was celebrated with great enthusiasm by all but me. I was dying from within with the burden of my heinous crimes. I hated myself and hated my newborn boy. And I hated myself for not loving my son even though it was not his fault.

It took me much longer to love that boy, to accept that belonging to a favoured gender was not his fault. He was innocent and ignorant about the fact that he was loved and preferred for his sex. He was naïve, scared, dependent, and a baby. It took me many months to ward off the hatred I felt towards him. When he got scared of the dark, when he called me from the washroom to be with him because a cockroach was approaching him, when he kissed me for making his favourite dish, or hugged me for picking him up from school, I realised he was not aware of the fact that he was loved by the conservative world for just being male.

The Guilt Never Goes...

ONCE WE had a patient with us since her fifth month of pregnancy, for poor obstetric history. She had had multiple abortions, ranging from eighth week to twenty-fourth week. We had admitted her from her twelfth week of pregnancy, placing a cervical stitch to hold her baby from coming out prematurely due to her weak womb. She was on bed rest. Her bed was in the corridor, from where every passerby could keep an eye on her. She was under constant supervision.

We were checking her vitals three times a day, as she had a history of hypertension in her previous pregnancies. She was being monitored for any signs of vaginal bleeding, urinary tract infection, or vaginal pressure. Greeting her in the morning and sending her off in the evening was our daily routine. As for her, she would share her everyday problems with us, and chat with us regularly. She was missed if we didn't find her on her bed in the morning, and we assumed she had delivered her baby at night. But just then, we would find her emerging from the toilet or being wheeled in from the ultrasound room. We wanted her to have a full-term baby,

not a premature one who would be confined to the NICU. Hence, we would be annoyed if she was seen walking around in the ward or corridor.

In her case, the chance of preterm labour was seventy per cent, and we were concerned that like most NICU babies, her baby would suffer from infections and other complications of prematurity. Moreover, her baby's growth was also restricted due to her high blood pressure. She was on antibiotics, anti-hypertensive medicines, uterine relaxants, and blood thinners. It was her fourth pregnancy. We were determined to give her a living, healthy baby this time, which explained our constant vigil on her.

During the delivery, we found the baby was in breech presentation, which meant its feet was down towards the vagina. We prepared her baby's lungs to breathe smoothly, by giving steroid injections to her. Blood units were booked for her in the blood bank. The senior consultant instructed us to call him any time, once she went into labour, or in case of an emergency. Standing orders were to issue blood and shift her to the OT as soon as any indication would arise.

Today her bed was vacant, I noticed upon entering the LR. The doctor on duty asked me to rush to the OT. The patient had been taken for emergency LSCS for labour pains, she said, and reminded me to take out the cervical stitch after CS. I ran to the OT, excited for her, but my heart kept racing with apprehension for the outcome of the surgery.

I was happy that she was delivering while I was on duty. I wanted to see the smile on her face once she held the newborn in her arms. Without bothering about other labouring patients, rounds etc, I rushed to the OT where my consultant

was scrubbing and waiting for me to assist her in the case.

The operation theatre was ready. Two paediatricians, one junior and one senior were ready with Boyle trolley, oxygen cylinders, nitrogen cylinder, neonatal resuscitation unit, and five pints of blood. We were confident about a successful outcome. Everybody was waiting for the happy moment nearing soon.

She recognised my eyes, though my face was fully covered in mask and cap. I expressed my wishes to her and gave a thumbs up sign by raising my brow. Her eyes showed her unquestioned faith in me. Our eyes were speaking the language of human compassion and love for each other.

'Shall we start?' the consultant asked the anaesthetist.

He replied, 'Most certainly, ma'am.'

A neat transverse cut given with scalpel was followed by Kerr's incision on the uterus. When the clear liquid drained, the baby's head was extracted, followed by its body. A nice loud cry filled the operation theatre. Everyone congratulated the mother and everyone else in the room. The theatre was in a festive mood. But we went back to the uterus, waiting for the placenta to come out. It was not separating, and the uterus seemed flabby, unable to contract. It would not expel the placenta, nor would it contract to control the bleeding. The consultant urged the anaesthetist to start blood transfusion and the injection named metheglin to help the uterus to contract. The woman wanted to have a glimpse of her baby for once, but the consultant asked the paediatricians to wait till bleeding was controlled. Too many people around the patient would distract the anaesthetist from doing his job. We noticed that the placenta was still stuck anteriorly onto the

uterine wall, in the lower segment. All measures were failing to stop bleeding.

'Let's proceed for hysterectomy,' the senior consultant ordered.

Two more units of blood were ordered, while another senior consultant from OT-2 joined us for the procedure of hysterectomy. To save her life was more important than saving her future fertility. However, despite the speed with which we worked in the OT, in spite of the full support of medicines, the bleeding at her placental site didn't stop. The placenta was piercing through the urinary bladder. Even after removing the uterus, the bladder base was bleeding continuously, obscuring the field of surgery. We applied multiple sutures, but still the constant flow of fresh blood was not stopping, diluted with saline water. The anaesthetist was pushing IV fluids and blood to maintain her blood pressure. We tried many methods, suturing, compression, warm pack, but to no avail. So, we decided to pack the bladder base with mops, put a drain and close the abdomen. We would remove the pack once bleeding stopped later.

A healthy 3.5 kg newborn was crying, inhaling his first breath and the mother, struggling with her last breath. The prognosis didn't seem good. Even after constant pressure, many packs were soaked within minutes. No other option was left now, other than packing the bladder base, clamping the cord, and leaving the adhered placenta inside. We knew the retained placenta would shrivel with methotrexate injections. Removing it would injure the urinary bladder. We closed the abdomen on pressed packs, and shifted the patient to the post-operative ward. She kept requesting to see her baby, but we wanted to wait, give her the chance to recover first and then comply with her wish. The senior consultant left after an exhausting surgery, instructing me to be with her. The senior anaesthetist chose to stay with her, as her BP was quite low and there was no urinary output.

We sat beside her bed, sipping coffee after a tiring five-hour long procedure. Our eyes were on the monitor, as her BP was still low, and there was no kidney function due to litres of blood loss. She was holding my hand loosely. Suddenly, I realised her covering sheet was getting wet with blood. On removing it, blood was seen oozing out from the stitch line. She was still losing blood from sputters inside, and we discovered that the packing was not effective. Her grip loosened and suddenly her BP was no longer being recorded on the monitor. We wheeled her to the OT hurriedly and called the senior consultant to see her. There was no time to give anaesthesia, and the doctor immediately cut open the stitches, and within moments, a volcano of blood and clots started pouring out. The bladder base was still bleeding profusely.

The patient was semiconscious, and we tried holding her up so that we would be able to save her. My consultant asked me to de-scrub and bring the baby from NICU. I could sense the failure of our efforts to save the patient. As fast as my legs would take me, I ran, climbed three flights of stairs, fetching the baby, carrying him to the OT as fast as I could. I nudged my drowsy patient to look at her beautiful baby. I helped her to touch his soft cheek. Her eyes welled up, and the pillow got wet from her tears. As for myself, my cheeks were burning in agony and my eyes turned red, trying hard to control my tears. Both senior consultants left, helpless and agonised, after

re-suturing her abdomen. We were around her, standing like mere spectators. Her eyes were looking at her baby wistfully, till they were open, but soon everything was dark for her and her son.

For six long months, she had stayed in the hospital, away from her family, waiting for this special day to hold her baby in her arms. She was confident about the treatment and care provided to her. She had left her body and soul in our hands, fully surrendering to the care of us doctors, believing in our competence.

On our part, we were well prepared for each step, including in the labour room, OT, and nursery. But God had different plans. Her newborn son was still in my arms, quietly moving his arms and legs. We doctors stood silently, some sobbing, some with bowed heads, witnessing her breath fading away. I felt she said to me to take care of her baby. I almost promised myself the same. We were sinking with her. We sat on the blood-stained, littered OT floor, dejected, inconsolable.

We kept the boy in NICU and handed it to the father once he was ready to take him. The bed in the corridor kept reminding us that God was all powerful and He could dispose of the proposals of humans at his own will.

This is how life goes on. Should we carry the burden of this guilt with every dying patient, reminding ourselves how limited our power is? All we can do is lend a helping hand; the reins are up in the sky. Our research, medical advancement, newer vaccinations, and drugs to prevent viruses, bacteria and cancers have limitations. God is showering newer kinds of sickness at a faster pace, compared to the growth of equivalent remedies.

During Covid, a life-saving drug Remdesivir worth ₹5,000 was being sold from ₹20,000 to ₹1 lakh per vial, and it soon became national news.

Many antiviral drugs were being hoarded and sold at exorbitant rates to dying patients. Oxygen, antivirals, ivermectin, Vit C or zinc all were being sold at black market prices. Though Covid was said to be a disease of the rich, after a year, it started mutating, making it more virulent and resistant to drugs. Most of these drugs were given as trials without first-hand experience of this new virus. It all started with the anti-malaria drug HCQ.

Though there were severe side-effects from its use, including gastritis, diarrhoea, loss of appetite, nausea, and constant headache, people started taking the drug prophylactically to protect the immune system even before they contracted the virus. HCQ, which was previously sold at dirt cheap prices, was suddenly the most sought-after medicine. People consumed it, developed gastric ulcer, and continued believing it shielded them from the virus. Then was the turn of antibiotics, azithromycin, doxycycline, cephalosporins to bask in the glory of a supposed cure.

Knowing the pulse of our patients now, we physicians started prescribing these drugs to all our patients with any symptoms whatsoever, including upper respiratory tract infection, mild cough and sneezing, mild fever, and so on. Even when we didn't want to prescribe these drugs, the recommendations were all over the internet, in every WhatsApp group, and more dangerously, the patients started consuming all these drugs without consulting doctors.

'Self-medication' was very much in vogue, inflicting more

injury to their bodies from antibiotics than from the simple flu or cold they had contracted. The strong antiviral drugs tocilizumab, remdesivir and ivermectin were found to be promising against the Covid virus, following small research. Without any big trial of its efficacy, it was out in public, hoarded, black marketed at thousand times its original price. Something similar was happening to oxygen cylinders, and oxygen concentrators, and nasal prongs.

However, after a few days, it was found that our immune system fighting with the virus sometimes initiates a strong cascade of events, making the host a victim to its own guard. The body fights back with an army of antibodies, white blood cells, platelets, a cavalry in full action that tries to kill a microscopic virus in our lungs. The smallest functional units of lungs are called alveoli. The alveoli are like flimsy, sponge-like, air-filled balloons. Air diffuses through these flimsy walls, in and out of each alveoli, wherein millions of alveoli make a large lung. We found out that if the walls of these tiny balloons are repaired after killing the virus, the lung walls are fibrosed, not allowing diffusion of air. The virus is killed; however, the battle is lost at the cost of a collapsed lung.

The human lungs, which diffuse oxygen and carbon dioxide through these permeable, flimsy, filtering membranes called the alveoli, are now healed with a fibrous structure. Our antibodies become our saviours, massacring the virus followed by healing and repairing of our own bodies. But healing the lung walls is not a good idea. Healed walls are impermeable to air.

So how about stunting the immune system to protect the lungs, the doctors and scientists discussed. Let's start some steroids to denude our immune system; it may help save our lungs; however, it was working as a double-edged sword. But how much, how soon, how long should it be given to protect our lungs and at the same time kill the virus?

On second thoughts, it was disclosed that if we started steroids at the height of viral multiplication, we might suppress our immune system to initiate a fight and that would be totally lethal to the patients. The virus would then get a chance to replicate and destroy our body after stripping our armour at the commencement, which was not a right strategy.

'Let's start steroids to dampen the destruction after first antibody response, before the immune cascade begins; that seems a better plan,' the doctors and scientists opined.

So as per studies, and with conscious deliberation, scientists and doctors decided to protect patients with steroids, which would start only after the antibodies fought their first battle, killing the batch of viruses.

The treatment and the dosage varied from one patient to another, as every individual would be reacting to the virus differently, presenting their complications at different stages of the disease. So, with the experience of treating many patients and studying the progression of the disease over several months, doctors kept modifying the protocols and therapy, tailoring them to match the people's response to the virus. Eventually, the worst of the virus passed off, leaving several mutations behind and also leaving doctors not much wiser than at the start of it.

A New Beginning

THE HOSPITAL building was beautiful, with spectacular interiors, fancy floors and ceiling, light grey walls, light brown wooden doors of the OPD, nice border on both walls leading up to the corridor, and with wall-mounted sanitisers outside every OPD chamber. There were English style paintings on the walls with thin, grey borders. The waiting lounge area had comfortable sofas, with a large centre table offering elite English magazines, and a big coffee table book. Harmonious sarod music echoed across the lounge.

At the reception desk, ex-hospitality staff from the hotel industry or former flight attendants had been recruited. The cafeteria served all exotic dishes packed meticulously, including fresh juices and espresso coffee.

The OPD chambers were huge, with awkward placement of tables and chairs facing each other as if in a living room. There was a computer screen and printer neatly placed on the table. Behind the curtain, was an automatic examination bed, examination light on the right side and a white marble counter with a wash basin, automatic tap, soap dispenser, and tissue paper dispenser with quality tissue papers in it. One could also see an electric kettle, white porcelain cups, coffee, tea, milk, two distilled water bottles in well-organised compartments in a wooden coffee tray.

The cupboards overhead were stacked with supplies—surgical blades, syringes, swabs, gloves among other knick-knacks and the ones below had disposable speculums, bed sheets, and tissue rolls. The huge glass wall facing the bed reflected sunlight, exposing us to the soothing green and blue of the natural world outside.

I wondered what weighed more around here, glitz and glamour, or compassion for the patients?

The day I joined here in Gurugram as a Director of Obstetrics and Gynaecology, I somehow felt something nag within me. Was I happy and content now? I was unsure, I felt out of place. All of it felt momentary and superficial. Hospital management people were sweet talkers, but one couldn't really make out their real intentions. It felt uncomfortable sitting on that chair in that chamber. The contrast between government hospitals and corporate hospitals was unimaginable.

Even today after many years, nothing has changed; a corporate hospital's management staff present themes with artificial smiles plastered on their faces. In the beginning, I found it difficult to force myself to come to this kind of workplace every day.

As a doctor, my soul had always been searching for meaningful engagement with my patients, as I went about treating their diseases and operating on them. Sitting inside a comfortable air-conditioned room seemed that I was wasting my skill as a doctor.

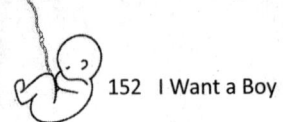

It took me a while to adjust to this new world and it brought with it a host of different experiences and glimpses of patients from the more affluent sections of society. I encountered some completely different kinds of patients in this new phase of my life, but here too, I found that some couples will go to absolutely absurd lengths in their quest for a male child.

Death is Always Tragic

THE PAIN a child has to endure tears a mother apart. Her worst fear is seeing her kids in distress. When they go through tough times, and deal with hardships, the mother cries in silence, as she is helpless to take their pain away. She comforts them, shows them a brave face, but deep inside she wants to protect her child from harsh reality. She cries because she cannot help it. A mother's greatest wish is to be able to safeguard her children from pain, illness, failure, and grief.

I wish as a mother, I had the power to protect my children till their old age. I plead with God to invest that power in me, so that my kids are raised in a safe environment. I wonder if Mother Nature is also helpless and unable to protect us. Is she silently crying too?

How can she be at peace seeing so many of her children dying and gasping for breath? The Supreme Power is rendered helpless too. We all had thought that her magic wand would take away every pain, but it cannot.

My message box had been full of requests for Covid beds, oxygen, ventilators, or antiviral drugs. Since morning there had been calls from known patients, relatives or neighbours pleading to arrange life-saving measures for them or for somebody in their family. I am a doctor ready to treat patients, but without resources how would I help? There was no bed, not even a ventilator, at the hospital. I had already refused pregnant patients in need of emergency delivery due to their positive Covid report. No one was ready to admit them.

I was feeling so helpless, being unable to help in deliveries of pregnant women, unable to help patients with fibroids with excessive bleeding, abnormal uterine bleeding, and unable to help my post-menopausal patients. We had stopped treating every sick patient. The corona patients admitted to our hospital were in a miserable condition. Our beds were all occupied; we had a non-functioning OT and several more failures.

Patients had started panicking. At the start of their first symptom of Covid, they were flooding their systems with every possible supplement, followed by drugs like ivermectin, antivirals, HCQ, antibiotics, blood thinners, low molecular weight heparin and steroids, with or without any doctor's advice. Prescriptions were literally floating through WhatsApp messages. Each possible medicinal formula was tested–herbal concoctions, Baba's Ayurvedic management, breathing exercises, steam inhalation till it would burn your nasal mucosa.

Treatment protocols were being abused left, right and centre, and the human body was not given enough time to start its own antibody response. Fungal infections of buccal mucosa, throat and eyes in its severest form were a common phenomenon because of the excessive and inadvertent use of drugs and steroids.

People were hoarding oxygen cylinders and concentrators,

selling antibiotics and antivirals at exponential profit margins. Patients were queuing up in hospital corridors and outside with masks on, some with their own cylinders, breathing heavily, waiting for hospital admission, and some even dying while waiting. The lucky ones who got admission were largely untreated too, as there was only one nursing staff for ten beds and she had no clue whom to help, or how to manage the chaotic mess.

Every now and then, a patient's condition would worsen, requiring resuscitation. The need for arranging ventilators or life-saving injections, and inhalers increased. It delayed the rounds; the nurses were not able to finish even the first set of orders given in the morning, and they had to skip their lunch time. The days merged into each other, with 48 to 72-hour-long duties as many nurses and doctors were also falling sick with Covid.

There was an inexhaustible list of patients requiring high-flow oxygen, with them being shifted to ICU and HDU. Then there were those unlucky patients who died every day. Patients lay dead, waiting in the ER corridor, even in the front lawn of the hospital. Their relatives waited for declaration of death for their death certificates, packing of the body and a certificate for the cremation ground without which burial or cremation of dead Covid patients would not be allowed. This went on for months. We knew that many of the dead people could have been saved. Many families were devastated, many children of young parents became orphaned. We were feeling helpless every single day. The stress was eventually numbing us from within.

Why hadn't we prepared ourselves for this crisis? Why

couldn't we foresee the scarcity of ventilators, hospital beds and other basic infrastructure? Why did we keep ignoring the call?

Was Covid like tuberculosis?

The latter was considered a deadly disease a decade ago and it still is. The tuberculosis ward is always a separate, isolated ward in hospitals. It is considered an infectious disease, spreading with contact. Most medical students have compulsory posting to a TB ward for a month.

Those days, we were instructed to observe full precautions, to wear cap, mask, and gloves before examining patients. The TB ward was always full to capacity, adding two to three active cases daily from the OPD. Patients were chronically ill, lying there for many months and were constant members of these wards. They would help new entrants with the methodology of taking TB medicines, and teaching them breathing exercises and precautions to safeguard others.

One of my MBBS batchmates, Dr Chavi was dedicated to her work. She was pursuing postgraduation in medicine from Agra Medical College. She was a thin, fair Himachali girl who wore thick glasses, and had a hunched back due to wrong posture from adolescence.

Dr Chavi was seen briskly walking to and fro with her notes, mugging them, memorising them with a constant humming sound. Sometimes, she would sit in the corridor, swaying her body back and forth, murmuring her notes in a stressed tone. Whenever she crossed our room in the corridor, that humming sound distracted me, disturbing my concentration. Once her humming faded, I would resume my studies. Once, I requested her to stop walking in the corridor, but she flatly refused saying that the corridor is a common area. She added that she didn't have time for petty discussions.

She was always burdened with those thick, enormous medical books. She was right; no one had time for wasteful, petty discussions, explanations, or fights. I collected my books and went upstairs and studied in my friend's room.

On the day of our viva, we didn't get to see her face; she was sitting in the canteen with a book plastered to her face. She had walked to the college with the book in front of her eyes, momentarily putting it down to recollect some important information. Upon reaching the viva room, she would spread her handkerchief on the floor and kneel, revising once again while her upper body would sway back and forth.

One of the boys asked curiously, 'Are you praying?' but she didn't pay any heed to him and kept studying intently.

Her topic for her thesis in her postgraduation was tuberculosis disease. She took it very seriously, as per her nature. She became an integral part of the TB ward, examining the patients, taking samples, collecting reports, maintaining data. Patients were also comfortable with her, reaching out to her with their trivial problems, as they knew she would take them seriously. The human bonding she shared with her patients fulfilled the purpose of her thesis. However, after a while she became careless in taking mandatory precautions in the TB ward and paid a price with her life.

As expected, this negligence resulted in her contracting a form of multidrug resistant TB. Due to her overexposure to TB patients who did not take their treatment and drug therapy as advised, Dr Chavi became an easy prey to the mutated bacteria, resistant to drug therapy, and stopped responding to treatment eventually. Her symptoms worsened despite taking ATT (anti tubercular treatment). She cleared her postgraduation exams and joined a government hospital in Delhi. But her cough and fever persisted, and her health was deteriorating. In her own ward, she was lying in isolation with her emaciated body, her lungs filled with water, coughing severely. The doctors, her professors and colleagues were helpless. They took her to many institutes for treatment, but eventually, she lost her life.

We all used to board the train to Gorakhpur from Delhi railway station in our MBBS days. Our fathers dropped us to the station every time. Chavi's dad used to come all the way from Chandigarh to Delhi to help his daughter to board the train and again to pick her up. This was the duty of our fathers, throughout our studies in medical college. He was not comfortable with the idea of his daughter travelling alone from Delhi to Chandigarh and back, even in a decent train. Every parent would have been waiting to see us, waiting to watch their progeny fulfil their dream, become successful doctors.

One day at the grocery shop, a familiar face was looking at me. He was Chavi's father, I discovered after a while.

'Oh yes, uncle, namaste! How are you? When did you shift here? How's Chavi? How's your younger son?' I asked. At that time, I was unaware of what had happened to her.

We all knew each other's families quite well after five years of being together. Chavi's father was a senior officer in the government. Her brother was just like her—fair, thin but taller than her, also with a hunched back. Chavi used to say that he was soft and introverted, and depended upon his sister for every decision or advice.

'Chavi is no more now. She finished her postgraduation in

medicine,' he said, his voice quivering.

I couldn't believe his words. 'What happened to her?'

He narrated the whole story of her postgraduation and how she contracted multidrug resistant TB.

He enquired about my well-being and I informed him that I had completed my masters in OBGYN, and also that I was a mother to a daughter. I knew it would make him sad seeing his daughter's batchmate leading a normal life, getting married and practising. Perhaps Chavi would have done the same by now, had she been alive. However, he smiled and asked me to bring my daughter along to his home.

'Your aunty will be pleased to see you and your daughter,' he added.

'How about your father?' he asked.

I turned around and said, 'He is no more.'

'Oh no, he was in good health, such a jovial person. What happened to him?'

'Cancer', I said.

'What type of cancer? Not diagnosed in time? We met three-four years ago, and he seemed fine then. He helped me a lot during your MBBS years! He would help us everytime with Chavi's train tickets and reservations. I had put this responsibility on him, and he took it happily. I was really upset about your frequent bunking of classes, but he explained that kids are facing a very difficult time in a totally new environment, and explained that we should let them find their way out to deal with this stress slowly. This frequent bunking will surely decrease as soon as they are settled in their studies. They were frogs from the well, and we have suddenly released them in the wide open sea. Our love, support, and understanding are what they are seeking right now to pave their path. I respected your father a lot. Such a good person, so sensible, practical, spontaneous with a hypnotic charm.'

He was all praises for my father.

I nodded and walked out with a heavy head, thinking about Chavi and the price she had paid for her negligence and diligence.

I was fatherless, and he was daughterless.

Witnessing the phenomenon of death as a doctor was now a part of my daily routine, and I would brace myself for it every day. But sometimes, some deaths of known faces, near and dear ones were too hard to bear, weakening my very core.

Often, I think about my father. Although, decades have passed, but no definitive treatment for cancer has been invented. We kill rapidly growing cancer cells with chemo and radiology, which simultaneously destroy our good functioning cells, causing severe side-effects like weight loss, hair loss, excessive vomiting, jaundice, decreased immunity, lung, and skin infections. Battling cancer is still painful physically, psychologically, and financially. It is an endemic of this new era.

Cancer is emerging like a bamboo shoot, rapidly destroying our society. Every single family has at least one member suffering with cancer. Diseases like HIV, Cancer, Ebola and now corona, are there among us to pose new levels of challenges every day. God is always many levels ahead of us, throwing surprise diseases at us. We keep on ducking, fighting, strategising, but eventually, it is man who finally loses the battle.

'YOU NEED to get Covid RTPCR test every week from now,' I told a patient who had completed her thirty-six weeks and was visiting to discuss her birth plan.

'The validity of the test is only six days; we will be repeating it till your delivery,' I added.

'Shall I get a test for my husband as well?' she asked.

'Yes, it will be required for your birthing partner too,' I replied.

'Doctor, I hope you are a Covid-free hospital, I mean you are not admitting Covid positive patients,' she asked again.

Till last year we were able to maintain the status as a Covid-free hospital; however, with this second wave, the number of cases had risen exponentially. One out of three pregnant women was testing positive for Covid, and beds in Covid hospitals were exhausted. For the same reason, the government had enforced the law to admit Covid positive patients in every hospital and nursing home to fifty per cent capacity. Every hospital needed to make arrangements for Covid, and be equipped with beds, oxygen, ventilator, and drugs.

We were dealing with our Covid positive patients ourselves and not sending them away.

'But doctor, we were under the impression that this is a Covid-free hospital. We are not comfortable delivering in here now. Could you please suggest some place where Covid patients are not being admitted,' the patient asked suddenly.

I tried to explain to her the gravity of the situation.

'Dear, if you yourself would have tested positive for Covid in a few days, would it be right to refuse admission to you, or ask you to go find another hospital at the eleventh hour and get your delivery done by another gynaecologist?'

'You might have to rush to a government hospital in that scenario, as no private hospital will take Covid-positive patients, risking their resources and reputation. We need to help our Covid patients, not steer them away just to maintain our so-called "Covid-free status".'

Moreover, if any hospital was trying to lure patients on this Covidfree tag, they would be punished. It was now mandatory for every hospital to make arrangements to treat Covid-positive patients, and we had seen that a negative report was not specific, as one could manifest symptoms and signs of Covid even after a few days of testing negative.

We had been monitoring symptoms of patients without relying excessively on RTPCR. Many patients were getting admitted with negative reports, delivering babies, and being re-admitted with fever, cough and breathlessness within a week of their deliveries.

In that grave scenario during the second wave, every family unit had at least one positive patient, some recovered, quarantined or admitted to the hospital. The news of distant relatives, and neighbours dying of Covid symptoms due to lack of oxygen, remdesivir or ventilator had become a common phenomenon.

A news channel showed the picture of a very young news anchor and journalist who had succumbed to death due to Covid. He had interviewed me for his channel on the topic of corona, only a couple of weeks ago. He was a young, healthy male with a good grasp on the subject and an authoritative voice, with clarity in his thoughts. His death was shocking news, but then, this calamity was all around us now.

Till last year, I was all geared up to help my patients, not leaving them if they contracted Covid, attending hospital daily, from morning till evening. The situation was manageable, but this year, during the 'Delta wave', when people were busy arranging oxygen and ventilators for their loved ones, I felt totally helpless.

I kept grieving for all my patients for whom I hadn't been able to provide any medical support. I felt worthless and felt like giving up practising; I felt like all I had left was knowledge and no resources.

I understood the patient's query about a Covid-free hospital, and why she didn't want to deliver in our hospital. I replied that we were taking all possible precautions, separate entry and exit, PPE kit, gloves, masks, and shield are being judiciously used, and so the patients need not worry.

'Tell me one thing, if accidentally someone ruptures her water bag and comes to the ER without a Covid report, what are we supposed to do,' I asked my patient.

'I don't know doctor, they should've gotten their test, it's highly irresponsible,' she mumbled.

'If she is just at thirty-two weeks?'

'I don't know, doctor,' she replied, hesitantly.

'Ok, so there is another ward where we keep patients with unknown status of Covid, but we wear PPE kits and maintain all precautions till their Covid report comes. Then we shift them either to the non-Covid ward or Covid-positive ward, as per their report. Thus, by maintaining this practice, we don't delay treatment for the mother or for her newborn, in case she requires emergency delivery or C-section,' I explained yet again.

'No doctor, I understand but still I don't think I am comfortable in this set up; I will go for a Covid-free hospital.

If you can come there and deliver my baby, it would be the best possible scenario, else I will have to settle for some new doctor, which will be psychologically challenging at this point,' she insisted.

Both of us excused ourselves for not being able to convince each other.

After ten days of this conversation, I got a call from her husband requesting me to admit her in my hospital post-delivery.

'Doctor, my wife delivered our baby in this great maternity hospital, but on the third day before her discharge from the hospital, she developed fever and infection. The doctor did the dressing and sent us home. It's been ten days that she has been Covid positive, so the doctor is consulting over phone, changing antibiotics to clear the infection, but the wound doesn't seem to be getting any better. A copious amount of discharge (pus) is oozing out from the wound. But they are not allowing her to enter the hospital or meet the doctor as it is a Covid-free facility.'

I was listening patiently to the contradictory behaviour which only humans are capable of, trying hard not to be judgmental or critical about the problem at hand but absorbing it calmly. It could have happened to anyone. I knew the hospital had denied medical care to her to promote itself as a Covid-free facility. Was it justifiable? I didn't have an answer; everything depended on the perspective.

How was I supposed to deal with it? Should I be annoyed? Should I refuse her, or take her in? Was I not clear enough to them in my conversation that such a situation might arise any time, as no one is immune to Covid?

Apparently, they were keeping themselves safe by staying at home, allowing no visitors, not going for walks or even to buy groceries, and hence they believed they could not get Covid. It was then that I had suggested such a scenario to the pregnant lady who was close to her expected date of delivery. I was basically guilty of scaring the patient.

However, I just wanted to explain to them that it was an everyday affair, anyone could have contracted Covid, whether symptomatic or not, so we should be prepared for it and take necessary measures and precautions. If despite taking precautions, someone happens to be Covid-positive, there was no need to panic as all of us doctors and staff nurses would treat them with care.

But no matter how much we tried to explain the situation, patients would get irritated and offended. They still felt that they were Covid-resistant as they were taking utmost precautions, taking their multivitamins regularly and staying at home since a year, protecting their bodies from the airborne infection.

The truth, however, is that no one is shielded. We have seen patients every day, not exposed to the outside world, still having severe lung involvement, in real advanced stages of the disease. Hence, we had urged our patients to keep their minds open in case they turned out to be Covid-positive during routine testing. It was important to be prepared, just in case.

In fact, more than eighty per cent cases were mild to moderate and recovered with simple measures. But because many patients were cocooning themselves in the bubble of self-assurance, they got upset if such a possibility was discussed with them, even well in advance.

Ray of Hope

'WE WERE thinking of an early delivery, doctor.'

Considering the spread of Covid in the city, the couple had arrived at this decision.

'No, it won't be advisable,' I protested during an ongoing online consultation.

Nevertheless, the patient went into preterm labour probably due to Covid fever. She was stable during the night. Morning the NST strip showed Foetal Bradycardia. Immediate measures were taken to comfort the baby in the womb, while the mother was shifted to her side in a left lateral position, and IV fluids were introduced to maintain her blood pressure for good perfusion of the baby, and intra-nasal oxygen was started for better oxygenation of the foetus. Still, the FHR remained below 100.

I ordered shifting the patient to OT for an emergency C-section in view of foetal distress. Her husband was called over the phone, to discuss the case virtually as he was Covid positive.

'Doctor, why are you delivering her now? You said delivery

can be detrimental for her health.'

'Yes, I said so, and it holds true, but I cannot ignore the health of the baby.'

'She might or might not require a ventilator. But the baby might die if we don't perform Caesarean delivery immediately,' I added, making him aware of the situation.

'No, I don't want you to deliver her as yet, I need to discuss this with my elders,' the husband replied, hesitantly.

'Sure, as you say, we are holding it as of now, and will do the surgery once we have your consent.'

The repeated calls from the OT to shift the patient if it's an emergency Caesarean were kept on hold until we got the husband's consent.

'Are you bringing the case in, or shall we take the elective case as posted in the list?' enquired the anaesthetist from the OT.

We couldn't hold the OT for long. It was wrong to keep the OT table and disturb the elective case list, so I released them from my urgent list.

I informed the attendant of foetal distress and how emergency delivery which was important to save the baby should not be denied. Then, I had gone for my morning routine rounds, which took some time. When I looked at my phone, there were 16 missed calls from various numbers.

I returned the calls; they were from the same attendant with many more queries.

'Can you handle it?'

'Do you have a ventilator? Does she have any chances of survival? Where will the baby stay after delivery? We both are Covid positive; all family members are recovering from Covid.'

All questions were genuine, but the answers were not known clearly. We tried to be as reassuring as possible, leaving a little room for clinical uncertainties. We tried to be empathetic, but not overtly emotional.

We knew we were holding on to a delicate thread; both ways, we might bear a fall.

In the delivery room, as we continued the surgery, we kept talking to keep our nerves cool, as the patient lay on the OT table.

'So how are you today? Is the baby moving, okay? I have started the Caesarean surgery, and the next sound will be the cry of the newborn baby.' I tried to strike a conversation to calm the patient down as well as, myself.

The baby was delivered, coated in thick meconium and we heard his feeble cry. We handed him over to the paediatrician. The tiny being was resuscitated soon, and his Apgar score improved. A shrill, loud cry of the newborn was heard by the mother.

'Oh, what is it, a boy or girl?' she asked.

'Congratulations, it's a boy!' the paediatrician announced. We continued our conversation while closing her womb and abdominal cavity. Contrary to our expectations, the patient withstood the surgery well.

I peeped through the divider between the operating area and the anaesthesia bay, smiled at her and asked whether she would ever be able to recognise me if we met without masks outside. We both laughed.

It was the first time after her admission that I was meeting her; all other consultations had been online. We talked about her love marriage, how her husband never left her side, how she got Covid. We conversed heartily to ease the tension and her apprehensions in the OT.

The baby stayed in the nursery for a day, recovered well and started on breast feeding, but under proper Covid protection guidelines. The incident was a ray of hope for all of us, after having been shrouded by darkness the whole year.

Doctor can Give You Life

IT WAS among my first emergency call days in this hospital.

A young girl of twenty, delivered an IUD (intrauterine death of foetus) baby after prolonged labour and was brought to the emergency. Her legs, her salwar, the bed sheet where she was lying—everything was soaked in blood. The lady supporting her was also wearing blood soiled clothes. She was put on a stretcher and the IV LINE was started. The monitor was attached, showing BP 80 systolic, pulse 120. Her abdomen seemed distended, and uterus seemed hard like a cricket ball. Her vagina was packed with gauzes, and blood was dribbling through them. We needed immediate blood transfusion for her to survive.

The patient was shifted to OT immediately for examination under anaesthesia. The surgeon on duty was called. All the gauzes were pulled out from the vagina, one by one, in anticipation of a sudden gush of blood. Our medical team was ready, and everyone stood in their respective positions.

We found out that there was no cervical tear, so the uterine cavity was curetted to check for any retained bits of placenta, which must be the cause of the uterine atony.

I placed my one hand inside the vagina and with the other, held the uterus like a ball and compressed it between my upper and lower hands. It controlled the bleeding, slightly. But on releasing the pressure, the bleeding started again. I stood in the same position, standing near her perineum, facing her hips with my back bent, arms aching, not able to relax.

The overenthusiastic surgeon was feeling neglected. 'Why don't we do hysterectomy to save her life?' he asked.

'But compression is showing good control of bleeding,' I replied.

'Still, this can't be the solution, standing like this, waiting for eternity.'

'No, if it doesn't contract, we can either do internal iliac artery ligation or uterine artery embolisation,' I replied.

Internal iliac artery ligation is a method, wherein we tie the blood vessels feeding the uterus on both the sides to stop blood supply to the uterus. Later, blood supply is restored by itself from the adjacent organs. But the surgery needs opening of the abdominal cavity, called laparotomy.

Her haemoglobin was as low as 2 gm, so there was no way she could take this surgery and come out alive. She might develop disseminated intravascular coagulation (DIC) cascade if she lost another litre of blood on opening her up. DIC kills the patient by multiple organ failure.

The best in this situation was the non-invasive way, clogging the uterine blood vessel with embolisation. The surgeon and I had a heated argument on the merits of saving the patient by sacrificing her uterus or saving the patient with her uterus. Embolisation was both ways the better option,

however it excluded the surgeon's role, his fee, and meant an unnecessary visit to ER in the middle of the night for nothing.

After the procedure, I had to stand for another six hours compressing the uterus between my hands. The very next morning, when I released my frozen arms around her perineum, bleeding was minimal. I had been bending for quite a long time, and I started feeling dizzy.

The next few days were crucial. She had developed fever, was bloated with retention, her kidney function was compromised, but she recovered in a week's time, and was ready to go home. Without sacrificing her uterus, I could save her life; it was a big milestone accomplished in my career. I was satisfied.

Also, it was quite a miracle when she conceived after four years again. Her uterus regained its blood supply from other organs' anastomotic blood supply. I have no idea if she was aware of the turn of events that night. She was just twenty and could have lost her womb at such a young age. A brave decision, a fight between doctors and the timely use of a medical technology flipped her life back to normalcy.

I RECALLED another day years earlier when my phone showed three missed calls from the same number. I picked it up the fourth time.

'Is this Dr Anu?'

'Yes, it is.'

'I am calling from Lifeline Hospital, Old Gurugram. I am the doctor on duty here. I need a favour. There is an emergency and I got to know about your experience in handling difficult situations. We have a child with bleeding PV; can you please come and see her?'

'But I don't attend to private patients. Where is your gynaecologist?'

'She is out of town, and she is the one who suggested your name. Please, the child had an accident; she is just five years old, and bleeding excessively; please come if you can.'

'Ok, call the anaesthetist, we will be doing EUA. In the meantime, please start IV line, and give her analgesia, and get an antibiotics test dose. I will be there in fifteen minutes.'

I informed my mother-in-law about the emergency and left immediately for the hospital, leaving my angel in her care.

Outside the hospital, I noticed an unruly crowd of labourers, frail and exhausted, in dirty, ragged clothes. Some were seen squatting on the floor, while some were standing around. A group of women with their children and men folk stood in a separate group. I hurried through the crowd in search of the duty doctor.

A little girl was sitting on an old gurney without any bed sheet on it. Her torn frock was soaked in blood. With her lustreless brown hair coated with mud, her tear-stained face looked distraught. I felt a surge of pity for her. The crowd was looking at me expectantly. No one dared to speak.

I asked for her father. A man from the crowd moved forward, and squatted with folded hands in front of me. I requested him to stand up.

'First tell me, what has happened to your daughter?' I asked him.

'Ma'am, while getting down from the tractor, a projecting iron sheet tore her private part, so she is not able to pee, and is bleeding profusely. Please ma'am, save her, please save my daughter.'

'Yes, we are here to do precisely that,' I assured him.

'But first, please sign on the consent form to allow me to examine her under anaesthesia.'

'No need doctor, please do it.'

'We need this. Please sign first,' I insisted.

'But I don't know how to sign,' said the illiterate father.

'Nurse, please take his thumb impression and shift the girl to the OT,' I said.

The little girl started crying, as she didn't want to be moved to the OT; she wanted her mother. I caressed her cheeks, offered her toffees from my bag, held her hand and tried to pacify her. But she started crying loudly, raising her outstretched arms towards her mother.

The mother, a pale, emaciated woman who was dressed in an old, tattered saree, held her daughter's hand. After a short while, she released her grip over her daughter's hand. The child again started to howl, but the mother let her cry because she was scared she would be scolded for delaying the medical procedure.

Our tiny patient was frightened of strangers, and seemed lost in this unfamiliar place. She feared the injections. She wanted her mother, who, she believed, would protect her from pain. The mother, on the other hand, seemed equally frightened of the unfamiliar surroundings, and fearful that her actions would annoy us. I asked her gently to accompany her daughter to the OT, and gave her a sterile gown to wear, so that she could accompany her little girl.

We wheeled the patient into the OT with her mother.

But the mother collapsed on the OT floor in shock, seeing the equipment inside! By that time, we had sedated our little patient, and she was calmly sleeping on the OT bed. We carried the mother into the pre-operative room and brought her back to her senses. She sat quietly, numb at the thought of what was happening. She sat with an uncertain expression as if in a foreign land, and as if she was dependent on others' mercy for her wellbeing.

The projecting iron plate from the tractor had cut through the child's perineum, cutting the vulva vertically from front to back. She was bleeding profusely. After removing her clothes, I got a better view of the wound. Thankfully, the urethra and vagina had been spared. I sutured her wound and dressed it aseptically, catheterised her, finally gesturing to the anaesthetist that my work was done, so she could taper off the anaesthesia. The girl soon regained consciousness and I patted her on her cheek.

As soon as she was up, she shrieked, 'Ma, Ma!'

The little girl was better. Her bleeding had stopped, and the infection was now controlled with antibiotics. We also gave her one shot of tetanus as a booster, as a precautionary measure. Her parents were clueless about her immunisations.

'Your daughter is good now. You will be able to take her home after a few hours,' I told her parents.

AT HOME, at supper, an interesting discussion started around the idea of opening a small hospital in a nearby rural area. Back in those days, Gurugram was catering to scores of surrounding villages. The local population would go to small nursing homes in their vicinity, typically run by nurses, who were some sort of registered medical staff, and had once worked as ward boys or technicians in a city hospital. With limited practical knowledge and no academic background, they were now practising medicine in rural areas.

The patients either didn't have money to afford a visit to a nearby city doctor, or didn't care who the doctor was. All they were looking for was some sort of relief from their ailment.

Wouldn't it be a noble idea to provide specialist care to the rural population under such circumstances? For a gynaecologist, wouldn't it be a golden opportunity to mint money? My father-in-law, a practitioner himself added that he would introduce me to the *dais* around and other compounders who could refer patients to our proposed clinic.

He was aware of how patients often lay in government Primary Health Care Centres (PHCs) without even being attended to, because of the pitiful lack of doctors in rural areas. Either the doctor on duty was on leave or was not interested, or had already started his own private nursing home. Moreover, they would shamelessly use the government's supply of drugs for the PHCs in their own nursing home.

My head was spinning. I thought if I started practising in such an area, would my competitors be nurses running hospitals, with a free supply of drugs, or patients based on commission? These were places without any standards of sterility or protocol. Even if I planned to charge the minimum after deducting the cost of sterilisation, autoclave, fumigation, the charges would be much more than other nursing homes. How could I beat this system and emerge a winner?

There seemed no point in continuing with the discussion and I retired to the kitchen to wash the dirty utensils.

Yes, I have heard of hospitals, nursing homes run by ANMs (Auxiliary nurse midwifery), retired nurses, and other non-medics. I have also heard of them conducting deliveries, abortions, female foeticide, and ultrasounds and other procedures of obstetrics care. These people have learnt to inject the most potent antibiotics used in intensive care units for simple PID (pelvic inflammatory disease, infection of uterus, ovaries, and fallopian tubes). I have heard of them conducting abortions for patients with 12-30 weeks of gestation, using their knowledge of medicines from the time they worked in hospitals or with doctors under whom they had worked.

With absolutely no respect for protocols, and ignoring all medical rules, they were freely using dangerous medicines on poor, unsuspecting patients. That is the reason why complications are so rampant in rural areas. Ruptured uterus, intestines pulled out of the vagina or obstructed labour with dead foetus, Vesicovaginal Fistula (passage of urine through vagina continuously), rectal tear, no hold on continuous flow of stool—the complications that could result were serious and life-threatening.

If disasters happened to their patients, these imposters would flee from the nursing home and hide for some months somewhere far from their hometown, till the heat died down and the news was forgotten. Then, these so-called 'doctors' would return to resume their practice by bribing the police, and once again commission middlemen or the local *dais* to bring patients to them when things went wrong.

They are making lots of money and their kids attend good boarding schools. Everybody in the system, from government officials to the local MLAs are fully aware of their activities,

but turn a blind eye to these wrongdoings.

I couldn't bring myself to understand why these hospitals weren't being shut down. I was feeling ashamed that I was unable to gather courage to serve these villagers who needed good, competent medical care.

A Witness to Complicated Marital Relationships

THERE WERE police officers standing outside my chamber, my coordinator informed me.

'There's a senior female officer and another tall male subordinate,' I was told.

'Let them in after this patient,' I told her.

The senior officer had visited me a few months before, I guessed.

'We have come for some clarification and some answers on official documents,' she told me.

'Yes sure, please let me know how I can help,' I replied.

'You have been summoned in this case, Somya versus Dr Rahul, second trimester abortion, three years ago. Please read the file before answering,' she said curtly.

I took the file from her, though I knew the case very well; the facts of the case were crystal-clear in my memory.

Somya was a dark-complexioned, average looking woman with loud, gaudy makeup, usually wearing big, printed dresses, accompanied by her middle-aged husband in pyjamas and flip flops. He seemed like a caring and loving husband,

his gestures seemed to be over-protective, for it was his second marriage and he desperately wanted it to work.

Somya was pregnant at the age of forty, and till sixteen weeks everything went well. However, soon after, signs of pregnancy-induced hypertension started. I suppose both wanted this baby badly to cement their relationship. They were seen in the hospital almost every week with some or the other concern, for an ultrasound, blood test or just to talk to me. They became friends with me, and with the ultrasonologist. Frequent ultrasounds were done to assess the development of the foetus, the amount of amniotic fluid, status of foetal kidneys in anticipation of complications due to maternal age as well as high blood pressure.

I got to know quite a bit about their personalities, their families, their previous marriages, and their strained relationship in the present due to the interference of parents and siblings. There were conflicts about almost everything, the brother, sister, parents, the lazy, non-existent dental practice of the husband, and so on. I would sit patiently, listening and absorbing all this during every antenatal visit.

Their case was a little too exaggerated. Her BP was high despite being on anti-hypertensive drugs, and then, her amniotic fluid had been decreasing from the sixteenth week onwards, and every week it got a little worse than before. The specialist of foetal medicine suggested amniocentesis, a test to detect chromosomal abnormality, Down's syndrome, or any other genetic problem in the foetus. It's very often seen in pregnant women with advancing age. But the fluid diminished considerably, and amniocentesis couldn't be performed successfully.

We waited for another week, and held counselling sessions with the couple, and with the husband's family. The wife's family could not come; her brother was fighting a divorce case, and was in jail with his mom, sister, and brother-in-law. In a subsequent ultrasound, we found that the amniotic fluid was absent. This was a dangerous situation, and there was no chance of survival of the foetus. With no fluid around the foetus, it develops Potter's syndrome. The mother's BP was shooting high despite two anti-hypertensive drugs.

Abortion of the foetus was the only way as there were no chances of its survival anyway. Her husband seemed to care about her health, and was concerned about the effects of high BP on her other organs. She herself, on the other hand, was apprehensive that she would not be able to conceive at her age again if this abortion happened. She was well aware of the non-viability of her foetus and her high risk of hypertension, yet she feared her marriage might get dissolved, as the baby was the only ticket to ensure a bond with her husband's family.

Something was going on in the family, which I didn't want to get involved with. They kept fighting with each other about the pregnancy, blaming each other in various ways. He cried on many occasions saying that he was misunderstood and that she was very difficult to deal with. He wanted this marriage to work as much as she did, and his mother also wanted to have a grandchild. But Somya's health was more important.

Hypertension-induced seizures, brain haemorrhage or cardiac arrest could cripple her for life. But Somya was in denial and felt the baby wouldn't have any chromosomal abnormality. She genuinely believed that she would escape from pregnancy-induced hypertension, despite being that old.

Finally, after a long battle, she was admitted to the hospital for the abortion. She kept on wailing that something wrong was done to her foetus. All of us were patient enough to support her; psychological counselling was done, her husband stood by her in the labour room, throughout her labour and delivery. The postdelivery period was uneventful. Her BP began normalising with only one drug, her urine output was good, and all other parameters improved within forty-eight hours.

Drugs to stop breast engorgement were given, and she was recovering well. The expelled foetus was taken to a foetal medicine expert, and a biopsy was taken for chromosomal tests, but the autopsy was refused by the couple. After two weeks, the report revealed that the foetus had trisomy triple X, and its survival was literally impossible. Trisomy X babies are physically and mentally challenged if they do survive.

After a couple of postpartum visits, they stopped coming, till one day, I got a message from Somya, 'I want to meet you to discuss why it was aborted; they are filing for divorce because of this.'

Somya texted me and visited my clinic. After a brief hello, she tried to remind me that she was my regular antenatal patient, and that she was ill-treated by her husband and his family.

'They forcibly aborted my unborn child, they poisoned me to kill my baby; they wanted to get rid of me,' she said.

'No, I don't recall any such scenario,' I replied.

After listening to her for over 20 minutes, I excused myself to see other patients. The next day, she was again in the waiting area wearing broad floral-printed pyjamas, dark brown lipstick, and foundation to conceal her dark, patchy skin. After I had seen a couple of patients, she entered and made herself comfortable, and began narrating her pitiful tale again from the beginning.

'They are not letting me inside the house. His mother never wanted him to marry, and he is a mama's boy. He is threatening me with divorce, and they won't give me compensation. They aborted my child without my consent, as I never signed the form. They had surely drugged me; I was not in my senses. Don't you recall how I cried and told you I was ill-treated by them?' She went on and on.

She also visited the ultrasound department, meet the foetal medicine expert, and requested her to revisit the report to see if the baby could have been saved. Then, she had asked for the foetus's chromosomal report.

Next day, her husband came to check if I remembered the case, and to let us know that she had filed an abortion case against them, which carry a non-bailable warrant. As a doctor, I understood the foetus was not viable as it had chromosomal abnormality and was destined to die. I remembered our detailed, week-long discussion till we were sure after repeated ultrasounds that it was an abnormal foetus. Thorough counselling was done with husband and wife, with both the foetal medicine expert and genetic counsellor before taking the patient up for mid-trimester abortion.

As per protocol, a consent form was signed by the patient and husband. Everything went smoothly—she delivered vaginally, the foetus was examined by our genetic expert and sent for further genetic testing, and finally the report confirmed abnormal chromosomal aberration. The patient was discharged, and the case was closed. But now, she had filed a case at the police station, and the officers outside were investigating the case.

'Do you remember the case?' the woman cop asked me.

'Yes!' I replied.

'In your opinion, the baby was not viable?'

'Yes.'

'Did she sign the consent form in your presence?'

'Yes!'

'Are you sure?'

'Yes!'

'But the consent form signature is not hers.'

I was shocked, dumbfounded.

'She could have changed it!' I said, disbelievingly.

'We have consulted a calligraphy expert and all her signatures on bank papers and everywhere else are totally different.'

'Okay!'

'Do you think her husband might have signed instead of her?'

'How would I know?'

'But you said she signed in your presence!'

'No, I meant she signed, but mostly our nursing staff gets all consents signed, so she signed in front of the nursing staff.'

'Then why did you say that she signed in front of you? It makes you a party in this fraud. Her husband is a doctor, do you know him, personally?'

'No!' I replied.

'Are you sure, no distant relation?'

'No, I had met him first time here as the patient's attendant.'

'In this consent form, you have countersigned confirming

it as the patient's signature.'

'Yes, we need to sign here as a routine. The sister gets patient's signatures and ours too.'

'But if it turns out to be a forged signature by her husband, you will also be culpable in this crime.'

'What? I mean how, and what benefit will I be getting out of it? There was abnormality in the foetus, hence our medical management suggested removal of foetus. Period. Where is the crime here?' I asked.

'Doctor, law is blind, judges need evidence, and evidence is directing that the patient didn't sign, and the signature is forged, and you have countersigned it. Even if the management is correct medically, you might be dragged into the case.'

'Oh my God, what next? What is the solution? If you can, please guide me.'

'Who was the sister-in-charge?' the officer queried.

'It was three years back! Almost all the staff is changed, replaced, or transferred. Let me check.'

I called the nursing superintendent, explained to her the situation, and asked her for the duty roster for that day, three years ago. She said, she would need to pull it out from IT which will take some time after permissions from the senior management.

'Okay, do it as fast as you can,' I requested.

Within a few minutes, the duty roster with addresses of all the nurses was in front of us. The sister-on-duty who took the signature was on maternity leave. We shared her address with the police officials for further enquiry.

The whole episode lasted for four hours. I had to cancel my appointments during that time and the entire experience left me disturbed and upset. No police team or legal official ever visited us again after that day. However, the strange episode remains fresh in my memory to this day.

Thrown Out by Second Husband

A LOWER middle-class couple from Punjab with a little boy of five years, clinging to the mother, was my next patient. I was smitten with the charming kid, by his voice, and his demeanour. He felt shy, a little frightened, and kept tugging at his mother all this while.

'It's okay, I don't get disturbed with kids around, let him be.' I tried to assure his father who tried to pull the child away from the mother every passing moment.

His wife was pregnant for the second time, with a history of epileptic attacks since childhood. Since the last few months, the frequency of the seizures had increased, and she had to be on sleep-inducing medicines. I suggested a consultation with the neurologist.

'Yes doctor, let's do that, I want her to be healthy; it is a very precious pregnancy,' said the husband, nervously.

'Every pregnancy is precious!' I said, wondering what the basis of such an arbitrary statement could be.

Anyway, after the antenatal examination, I prescribed supplements and advised a few tests, asked to consult the neurologist and to revert with all the reports. He helped her get up, though she clearly didn't need any help, and the boy tagged along, holding her *kameez*. I was loving this innocent little son of hers.

Time passed and on her next consultation, she came alone with her son.

'Hi, are you going to school? What is your teacher's name?' I asked the cute little boy.

'No, he doesn't go to school,' the mother replied.

'Why? He is five!' I was surprised.

'His father doesn't admit him in a school. He says we cannot afford it.'

'But you are coming to this big corporate hospital for check-ups. I can't believe a small neighbourhood public school can be costly for your family,' I couldn't help saying.

'He doesn't listen to me,' she said.

'But he can't destroy his son's life like this,' I blurted out.

'It's not his son!' she replied and paused.

I was shocked for a while; I wasn't expecting this. They seemed like a happy middle-class family, like many other families around us. I learned that it was her second marriage. Her first husband had died in a road accident, leaving her alone with this young three-year-old boy. The dead husband's family apparently didn't want her there. She was married off to a childless divorcee. Initially, he loved her a lot, cared for her son as his own, but then started to demand his own biological child to carry on his legacy.

On his sudden whims, he would stop her epileptic medicines and hurt her boy, whenever she tried to protest. In her semiconscious state, she would witness her son being beaten, starved, and crying. It was unbearable for a mother, so she stopped protesting. She tried to contact her brother too, several times, but in vain. He was burdened with his own responsibilities and couldn't offer much help.

And then one day she conceived, and circumstances changed, not much for her son but for her. Now she was getting medicines on time so she could take care of her son too. She was not sleepy or drowsy. She fed him well as she was getting proper healthy meals. The little boy, however, was abused many times for getting a share from his mother's plate of meat, fruits and dry fruits.

'How can you stay with such a person? Reach out to NGOs, or I will help you in contacting them; you can work and raise your kid. Please don't carry on with it, at least think about your son's psychological state, no education, no love, all abuse, and neglect. How can you put up with it, and why should you? You are still at a very early stage of pregnancy. If you do not want his baby, you have every right to discontinue this pregnancy. The husband's signature is not required by the law,' I suggested.

She was sitting, staring at the wall, and then uttered feebly, 'But I don't have money to buy these abortion medicines.'

'I have free samples if you want.'

'I don't want to live with him or, carry his baby, but what choice do I have? I don't earn, so how will I feed my child, or myself?'

'You know, there are female support groups, NGOs and female police—anyone or everyone will help you, please get out of this sad relationship for your son's sake,' I said, trying to convince her.

In her subsequent visit, she looked a little determined. She took the tablets from me. It was explained that these tablets are to be taken in early pregnancy, else they won't work. I left it to her to make her own decision.

She vanished and didn't return for long. It was her seventh month of pregnancy, when she visited me with a pot belly in front and husband beside her.

I didn't ask her anything, and she herself began talking.

'I couldn't do it doctor, I didn't find time. I forgot how to take the medicines; I was afraid of bleeding,' she confessed guiltily stating an excuse.

I kept quiet. I simply examined her and instructed her about supplements and proper food.

On her day of delivery, she gave birth to a baby boy again, and he was born naturally through her birth canal. Sweets were distributed in the labour room, nursery and OPD wing. The father looked so happy and proud. She was exhausted and needed some rest.

The next day on my rounds, the father was feeding the baby with a bottle as she was too weak and tired. I preached on the merits of breastfeeding and encouraged the mother to nurse the newborn, and on that note, I congratulated her, reminding her to visit me after a week for a postpartum check-up. She never came back.

Time passed. It had been several months since I had seen her. One day, when it was time to rush to the OPD after rounds, I stopped suddenly, noticing her sitting with her son in one corner of the OPD area. I walked up to her, but she seemed a little uncomfortable.

'Hi, how are you?' I asked.

'How's your younger son?' I asked again, smiling, while picking up her elder son and placing him on my lap.

'He is with my husband.'

'So has he gone to get medicines?'

'No, he has left us. We have been forced to live on the pavement. I don't even have the money to go back to my brother. So, I came here seeking your help.'

I was aghast. Was it all for real? I couldn't seem to believe this. Was she fooling around with me? But I wanted to help her genuinely. I requested the OPD nurse to hold the patients for a while, while I took her inside my chamber and asked for her brother's phone number. He said it would take him two days to reach there, and till then he requested me to take care of his sister. She didn't want any shelter, food, or help from NGOs. She only needed money for a few days till he arrived.

Again, I didn't hear from her after that day. I kept hoping the help offered to her was enough till her brother came and took her.

Abortion and Summons

IT WAS Sunday. I often went for my morning OPDs on holidays as well. A call appeared from a landline number on my mobile. Usually, I don't pick random calls, but this time, I was free and took the call with a casual 'Hello'.

'I am calling from Lucknow Police Department and wanted to meet you as soon as possible,' someone said in a firm voice.

Taken by surprise, I replied, 'Ok sir, but why do you want to meet me?'

'It is a case of abortion under you in dispute. I won't take much time... I can come right now if you are free.'

I tried to collect my thoughts. I was dumbfounded. I couldn't remotely connect any case with this call. However, I needed to meet him urgently to know what the dispute was about and how I could possibly be involved. I also needed to know how I could get out of it as soon as possible. As doctors, we are always scared of medical negligence cases against us.

In recent years, it has become a pastime for lawyers and an easy way to earn money. They latch on to grieving attendants, dig into medical files, and then concoct stories about gross mismanagement and negligence—the list just goes on. But the truth is—however much we try, filling consent forms, signing and countersigning, sometimes even we become lax; we leave the mundane tasks like form signing to junior doctors and nurses on duty. We become gullible in such situations and believe that the paperwork was all done, until one day, a patient comes back, out of the blue, with the court's summon that the doctor in question deliberately misinformed him or her, didn't take consent, or took consent for something else, altogether. That explains why most of the time, when we are suspicious of a patient's intent, we ask them to write their consent in their own language.

I called the police personnel to the hospital OPD.

In my anxious brain, the clock was ticking and thoughts were spinning around my troubled consciousness. I tried to figure out in my mind which case it was that the police were enquiring about, and blamed myself for not making it a habit to check consent forms.

After checking on the third patient, I came out of the room, to find him sitting in the waiting area calmly.

'Oh, you have arrived, why didn't you call me? I was waiting for you inside,' I remarked.

'I know, doctor, but you were seeing patients, and I didn't want to disturb you.' He was so polite and respectful, in stark contrast to the image of a policeman I had in my head.

I invited him into my chambers.

He was in his khaki uniform, with epaulettes and badges on his shoulders and on his chest. He wore a wide, copper-coloured belt, black shoes, and a hat, which he removed and

was carrying in his hand as a gesture of respect. He took out a paper from his file and handed it over to me. It was a summon from the Lucknow Court, enquiring into the case of Mrs Mitali, wife of Mr Kuldeep who had wrongfully aborted their heir.

'What is this? Why would I abort someone's baby?' I asked, in shock and bewilderment, seeing the contents of the summons.

'Let me see,' I added, and read the summons in detail, but couldn't place the patient in my memory.

'Don't worry, we know that you didn't do anything wrong. It is a divorce case—husband is not ready to pay alimony to wife because she aborted his child. Now wife is blaming you of wrongful abortion.'

I prayed in my head that the consent form should have been signed; otherwise, my life will be ruined, my years of practice as a doctor, my first and last love 'medicine' will slip away from my life! I won't be able to see patients, operate on them, deliver little babies. What's worse, my kids would hate me forever, my family would accuse me of carelessness and that thought itself crushed me from within.

'Doctor, can you please let me see the file, and consent form?' the policeman asked.

I was brought back from my nightmarish string of thoughts which was plaguing me already.

'Today is Sunday, let me check. The Administration department is closed on Sunday.'

I called the medical record department enquiring if anyone could help. A person was there, but he didn't have the key to the filing section. I requested him to provide me with

the number of the concerned person. This fellow measured the gravity of the situation and asked me to come to the office immediately and stayed with me till the file was found, then waited to take it back to deposit it safely.

Both the officer and I wanted this to be over today, itself. After all, he had taken great trouble to visit all the way from Lucknow, and my troubled train of thought had to be halted. The file was opened. There were four consent forms, much to my relief! I finally breathed deeply, and the tension lines on my forehead eased for the moment. I remembered this patient in an instant!

My friend and colleague from the psychiatry department had called me one day saying she was sending a patient who was on antipsychotic medicines for two years and had conceived. But due to dangerous side-effects to the foetus, the woman needed an urgent abortion. Moreover, my colleague explained that her disease was acute with a history of a suicidal attempt once and other instances of self-neglecting behaviour.

Her mom brought the woman to me. She was a fair-complexioned, thirty-six-year-old wearing a nice, light-coloured embroidered suit with an elegant dupatta. However, what struck me was her unkempt hair, her worn-out slippers and an expression of anxiety and doubt written all over her face. The mother of the woman also seemed confused, unkempt, and restless.

They both started talking together, one interrupting the other mid-sentence, asking the other person to stop. Finally, the daughter won, and the mother gave up.

'They married me off to this rich person in Lucknow. I have always lived here in Delhi; I cannot live in such a remote

city. I studied in Delhi University. I feel suffocated there. They are very conservative. He loves me, and I love him a lot, but I can't live there. I requested him to come to Delhi, but he won't! Why can't he come here? I fail to understand that. We both love each other, then why does a girl have to move with her husband as a rule? Why can't he come with me, instead?'

Her mother tried to reason with her, saying, 'Darling, his business is established there, and he is the only son. Why don't you understand? Try living there, you would like it; do some job; it is a great big city, not a small town. You hardly stayed there after your wedding, always running back to us. Now your father has also passed away. You need a home, a family. For how long will I live? He cares for you, loves you, don't do this stupid act.'

I was watching as a silent spectator, trying to make sense of the conversation.

'So, what's the matter?' I asked.

'Doctor, please tell me whether she should continue this pregnancy or not,' the mother asked.

'As per the explanation of her psychiatrist, both her suicidal tendency and her medication can be detrimental to her growing baby. But if she still wants to continue with her pregnancy, we are absolutely with you. We will make sure that you and your baby remain healthy,' I replied.

'But I don't wish to continue, I have my own dreams and aspirations. I studied Economics and don't wish to ruin my career in Lucknow. I can't take this responsibility! If he doesn't shift here, I will abort this child,' the daughter said, quite unapologetically.

I was a mere spectator. So, I played my role accordingly.

'Okay, ladies, I think you need to discuss this matter at home, she is at a very early stage of her pregnancy now, and you have another four weeks' time to think about the option of abortion. Let me know then. We are here to help you either way with a team of obstetricians, psychiatrists, and clinical psychologists.'

'No, no, we have decided, I want an abortion.'

'Yes, even I feel she is not fit to go through the pregnancy with her present physical and mental health,' her mother added.

'I understand your point, still I would want both of you to take some time to reconsider your decision, because destruction done once cannot be undone,' I warned.

'In case your decision regarding the abortion is final, we need a letter from her psychiatrist stating her mental condition. After all, drugs might be harmful for continuing pregnancy. A letter from the clinical psychologist is also crucial at this point, stating that she cannot take the right decision in this state, so her mom's consent would be valid. We would also need a letter from her mom, stating her formal consent for abortion (it should be in her own words and language).'

I was very clear about the requirements and formalities regarding the procedure.

After a week, both mother and daughter visited me for the second time, and the drama started all over again. After a series of blame games, anger, indecisiveness, they finally showed two prescriptions, one given by the psychologist, and the other by the psychiatrist, as asked for.

The procedure was scheduled for the next day, and a routine consent was taken, signed by both the patient and her mom.

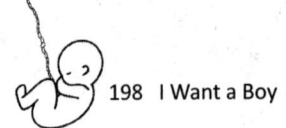

The abortion was done quietly. They left after a day's admission, never to be heard of till today, through the court's summon that I had wronged her, and aborted her child.

After seeing all the consent forms, the police officer assured me that her husband is a powerful man but a kind fellow, and that he would never let any harm be done to me.

He explained, 'His anger was against the girl's family. They got their mentally ill daughter married to him without disclosing her condition before marriage. As for him, he still wants to continue with it, but she is demanding separation and alimony, which he is not willing to pay. From the beginning, he has been suffering and now he wants her out for good. I am sorry for troubling you on a Sunday. Thanks for your cooperation,' the police officer said reassuringly.

Model's Hysterectomy

A VERY beautiful girl with radiant skin and an hourglass figure entered my chamber along with her husband and mother. She was dressed in an elegant *salwar kameez* and flowing dupatta, and I noticed her lustrous hair, her big, ocean-like eyes, and her full lips. She looked attractive, yet there was something very artificial about her appearance. The husband, on the other hand, wore torn jeans, and looked far from decent. The mother with her broad nose, dark skin and lips, and plain face looked nothing like her daughter.

The girl seemed frustrated with her irregular menstrual bleeding, continuing for months, which needed to be controlled by progesterone (hormonal) treatment. Her bleeding, after every ten days, moderate to heavy, was depleting her of her haemoglobin. She was a model, and it affected her work, and her energy to perform on a regular basis. But if she took progesterone to stop bleeding, she said it would take a toll on her looks. There would be bloating, eruptions of acne, hair fall, and she could not afford any of that.

Upon knowing her medical history I learnt that she was on

isotretinoin medicines for her skin, which was initially started for acne, but the drug proved to be a boon for her. After just a few days of using the medicine, her skin started glowing like the morning sun, and her modelling career took off with aplomb. But though she couldn't stop the medicine now, she wanted to get rid of her uterus because of the continuous bleeding. It was hurting her physical and mental health. She and her husband had decided against having kids anyway, so that wouldn't be a problem.

Her mother, on the other hand, started crying for her daughter's poor health; she wanted her daughter to regain her health, kids, or no kids, career, or no career.

'Do you have an ultrasound report? Let's see if you have some polypoidal growth, fibroids or something which might be causing this,' I probed.

'Nothing has been found in the reports, doctor. But I know I am suffering.'

'When was your last Pap smear done?' I asked.

'Never, I haven't even heard about such a test,' she said, sounding clueless.

'Okay it is a screening test for the mouth of your uterus, also called cervical cancer screening test. It detects any kind of abnormality or infection in your uterus. We can take Pap smear once uterine bleeding stops. And let's get a fresh ultrasound of the uterus and ovaries. We need a few more investigations to check the cause of your poor blood clotting, and also to check the functions of your liver and kidney. We will meet after a week with these reports,' I clarified.

'Okay doctor, please save me, I cannot live like that. Take as many tests as possible, but resolve my problem. In the meantime, what can I take to stop the bleeding?' she asked, sounding desperate.

As she wasn't interested in taking progesterone, I prescribed a tablet, a tranexamic and mefenamic combination.

'No doctor, it doesn't suit me. I am not allergic to it, but I have irritable bowel syndrome, so digestion is a problem. I cannot eat many things, I am literally starving since years. My intestines revolt and I start intestinal bleeding instantly. I am undergoing treatment with a gastroenterologist for this. And no medicine will suit my gut,' she explained.

'Is there anything I can help you with? Would you like injections to stop your estrogen-progesterone production? It is effective for a month till we figure out what's going on in there,' I said.

'No, I don't think it's a good idea. I am not comfortable with this. In fact, I am sick of taking medicines with all their side-effects. I am like a lab rat for doctors. Now I am exhausted. I want my uterus out. I love my work, and I will live for my passion. I have no desire for a family or kids.'

'I can understand your frustration. Let's meet with test results as soon as possible and try solving the puzzle of your irregular bleeding.'

I thought of every possible cause of abnormal uterine bleeding, until the truth hit me. I knew the drug isotretinoin was the culprit. I was sure many doctors already had told her about this, but she was not ready to hear it. The drugs were apparently magical for her skin and her career, and she didn't want to discontinue it. She was instead willing to lose her uterus, her fertility and worse, bring on the onset of early menopause.

I didn't mention all this as I wanted to give her the benefit of the doubt. What if she had an illness and we were not able to find out. She needed a second chance. She had researched a lot about me on the internet and had travelled a long distance for an answer. She appeared relieved after our first discussion.

It took a while for me to understand which drug would suit her, given her weak intestines. Centchroman biweekly, Mirena insertion, GNRH injections, were some of the options, while endometrial ablation, uterine artery embolisation were among the options I personally had for her. However, my methods were more conservative, as I wanted to save her uterus instead of going for a hysterectomy.

Both husband and wife visited me several times afterwards. Reports came as normal, but any treatment offered to her in the form of oral medication, according to them, would affect her gut or face, without stopping her bleeding, though her haemoglobin was normal. I couldn't locate any acne on her face which, she said was concealed with heavy makeup, but I couldn't see any evidence of it.

'Are you scrutinising your face with a microscope?' I joked.

Then I added, 'The continuous bleeding has had no effect on your iron levels or haemoglobin. You must be taking good care of your diet.'

'Yes, I am doctor, it is all healthy and green.'

I tried to make her understand that the skin medicine which she had been using for years might be the reason for her irregular bleeding. It has many more serious side-effects so why don't we stop this for a while to see if it works?

'And if the culprit is found, you will be free of all sickness, your intestines would breathe, your menstrual cycles would resume to normal flow. Let's give it a try.'

'No doctor, I have done that before and found that rebound acne and bad texture ruins my face. I cannot afford it,' she remarked.

All she cared about was removing her uterus. It was not easy to convince her that it wasn't a good idea. The girl was confident that I would be the best surgeon for her hysterectomy, as she knew I was skilled in laparoscopic surgery.

'Please doctor, take my words seriously. I want this out and I want to move on with my career. It is affecting my career; I am losing many assignments due to constant weakness and bleeding.'

No amount of counselling helped us arrive at a more acceptable treatment option. Radical removal of a twenty-eight-year-old woman's uterus seemed so wrong especially when I knew that her uterus was not at fault. Her womb was perfectly normal, only reacting to the constant onslaught of a wrong drug.

'It's been three months now doctor, let's settle with the most practical option. I don't want any temporary way to handle it. I want a hysterectomy, agreed to by me, my husband, and my mother. I think you should accept that and proceed with the surgery as soon as possible,' she said quite stubbornly.

'Sure, let me request one more thing, I will be needing a psychiatrist and a clinical psychologist's prescription certifying your sound mental condition. It will be helpful,' I replied.

I didn't hear from her since then. Such is the nature of my work; I encounter many patients with weird attitudes, unusual histories, and stories, but I take them all in my stride.

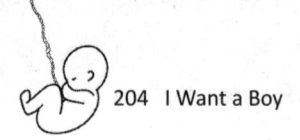

I Want a Boy

WE HAD entered the festival month. It was the festival to get a baby boy. In one of the labour rooms, the ceremonious fervour had started even before delivery. The labouring patient was enduring her pains silently and all others around her were happy and cheerful. The mood was rife with anticipation. A number of gift bags were lined on the table, including stacks of sweets boxes, jewellery boxes and gift envelopes with money were neatly named and displayed.

It was going to be a boy this time. It was confirmed with an ultrasound abroad, without any doubt.

'It is my youngest son's, doctor,' the patient's mother-in-law exclaimed with pride.

'Both my elder sons have sons. Poor boy, he had two daughters in succession. My heart cries seeing him without an heir. But this time we made sure that she carries my grandson. We have confirmed it multiple times. You wouldn't believe, it cost us twelve lakhs to get the whole IVF procedure for a test-tube baby done in Thailand.'

'First male baby didn't survive beyond ten weeks of pregnancy. Hence, they asked us to be under medical care till completion of twelve weeks. IVF itself is exorbitant in a foreign land, plus the lodging cost for three months—all for my son to get a son.'

'What is the use of all this money if we don't have an heir? We need a boy to inherit it, propagate it. Girls will go away to another family; boy is yours for forever. Look, how innocent my son is, one after another girl broke him from inside. He was losing interest in business, in himself, in family. He was going into depression.'

'It was very difficult to convince our daughter-in-law to

agree for this IVF. She was stubborn. She is a self-absorbed person, without any concern for my son's mental or physical health. According to her, two kids are enough, and she will be mocked for producing a third child, she claims.

'According to her, the boy is not necessary in today's world when girls are soaring high in every field. How much we had to plead with her for this last chance. That's why the need for a sureshot, foolproof, hundred per cent formula to have a baby boy was searched and researched. Many of our relatives endorsed this hospital in Thailand for selective boy pregnancy.

'Today, I have invited my brothers and their family, my daughter's extended family and her parents. I don't want to waste a minute to distribute all these gifts on arrival of my grandson. We have been shopping for months for this day. Gold jewellery for everyone with saris and sweets.'

The enthusiasm was bursting from every vein of hers. Her heart was pounding with this expectation of good news.

I turned towards the labouring patient. We exchanged smiles, hers a little embarrassed, strangulated, and fearful and mine, a little encouraging. She was silently bearing her pains. She had gone through this before. Every painful contraction was tearing her pelvic bones which she was absorbing with resilience. I did her pelvic examination and requested everyone to wait outside. However, her mother-in-law stayed. She didn't want to lose sight of the boy who was about to be born, even for a few minutes!

The labouring patient was positioned, delivery trolley was ready with instruments, paediatrician in position, and nurses holding her up with words of encouragement. After a couple of good strong pains, the baby's head was seen and the minute it

popped out, it was crying instantaneously for breath, followed by the delivery of its slippery body with another contraction.

Everyone was knocked speechless at this turn of events. They were dumbfounded and bewildered.

The labouring patient got worried. She knew something was wrong the minute the excitement died out in the room. The mother-in-law fell on the floor with a thud. The nurse helped her to sit up and offered her water, and checked her blood pressure. Everyone else stood around with bowed, sullen faces.

'Congratulations, it's a daughter,' announced the paediatrician to the new mother.

He had no clue of the background history of this case. The paediatrician wrapped the baby and brought her to the new mom.

'Remove her clothes, let me see her genitalia,' shouted the mother.

'Remove her clothes. It can't be true. Check it again, please. It was a boy, it was supposed to be a boy, it was checked by ultrasound multiple times. Please check correctly, doctor, please.'

She went silent and comatose thereafter. She never responded on my rounds when I asked her how she was, if she had pain in the stitches, if she needed any help for breast feeding or psychological counselling.

On her follow up visit after seven days, all hell broke loose. She cried in my arms, inconsolably. Thenceforth, she slowly regained her confidence.

Ayesha's Shattered Dream

'GOD PLEASE deliver a baby boy this time.' I requested the nurses, the doctor on duty, and the paediatricians to pray for Ayesha.

I remember how this patient, Ayesha Ali was crying when she first came to see me.

'Life of a girl changes after marriage,' she had said.

'How could I ever believe that fate would betray me? How happy was I when I was pregnant for the first time. I was given such a royal treatment. We were consulting the most reputed and expensive gynae in the city. My sister-in-law on the other hand, was going to some unknown gynae. But we are rich and affluent and hence, didn't feel like going to a doctor with an average practice. I delivered a baby girl by Caesarean section. We were happy about our first-born, a daughter.

'My sister-in-law delivered a baby boy through normal delivery. For my next pregnancy, I visited her doctor for a normal delivery and to ensure that I deliver a boy as well. I delivered normally but it was a baby girl again and around the same time, she delivered a baby boy.

'I was pregnant once again, desperate to have one baby boy. She also conceived thrice. We both delivered normally with the same unknown doctor who now had a bigger practice. She gave birth to a baby boy; and I gave birth to my third baby girl.

'I was shattered, heartbroken. Why wasn't I able to give birth to a baby boy? My own sister-in-law was teasing me by delivering a baby boy one after the other, close to my own deliveries, to rub salt on my wounds.

'Every time, she would say, "Oh, I wanted a baby girl this time!"

'I was dead from inside; from morning till night, I would think about my longing for a baby boy. I was the object of pity in my in-law's family.

'Oh, that Ayesha who has three daughters! Don't go to her house to congratulate her because she has delivered a girl again, what bad luck. On the funeral of my father-in-law, every guest was consoling me and my mother-in-law as I did not have a baby boy; it seemed that the untimely death of my father-in-law due to cancer didn't matter at all. I was constantly abused by my mother-in-law, and my daughters were cursed daily,' she said sadly.

'God, please give me one son to put a stop to everyone's accusations and hatred towards me and my daughters. I was fumbling, lost in my own agony, unable to concentrate on my daughters' food, health, and studies,' said the young woman.

'I was transformed. I was very fair with sharp features, flawless skin, and attractive figure. People were jealous of my beauty. Now, I can't recognise myself. In the mirror, I see dark pigmentation over my nose, both cheek bones, and at the centre of my forehead. I see my sunken eyes with dark circles

around, my wrinkled skin, disfigured shape, lax muscles. It is not me. I used to have a taut tummy, thighs, and full cheeks. I loved dressing up in expensive suits. How many times my sister-in-law had borrowed my suits and dupatta, only never to return them.

'I will try once again for a boy. It will be my last chance to reclaim my life. God cannot be that cruel. This time, he will grant my wish, I said to myself. And I was pregnant again!

'As the date of delivery was approaching near, I was losing faith in God. What if it is not a boy again? I did not go for regular visits to my doctor, this time. I was not able to feel anything—the anticipation was killing me, draining whatever was left inside me. The boy would be my elixir; he would give me back my life, my self-respect, the purpose of my existence, and win the love of everyone back for my neglected daughters.

'They are so innocent, I love them, I want them to look good, dress up nice, excel in studies. But for all of this to happen, I needed a son. Or else, we will be treated badly in the household.

'God, grant me a son this time. My mother-in-law took me to a cheap, local doctor. 'This time, we have no money for your delivery, each one of your daughters cost us ₹70,000. We are broke delivering your daughters," she reminded me in a harsh tone.

'No, I want to go to my doctor; the same doctor who once was a small name, but she has been delivering all my babies,' she insisted to her mother-in-law.

'I told my mother-in-law that I would request my doctor to consider my case for pregnancy and if possible, give some concession or discount. I couldn't imagine delivering my baby

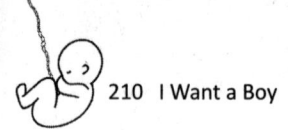

in a filthy, small nursing home. "What if it is a high-risk case in my fourth delivery, with postpartum bleeding, rupture of uterus and some other complications?" I told my mother-in-law.

'As much as I wanted a son, I want to live for my daughters, otherwise I know no one will take care of them, my innocent kids will be ruined by this cruel world.

'Please deliver my baby, doctor; I feel safe with you.'

Ayesha's words and her story pierced my heart. How much I had to plead to the management to make an exception for Ayesha and decrease the delivery charges for her. And how much I was praying for her to deliver a baby boy.

'Push, Ayesha, push!' I urged.

I wanted to close my eyes and did not want to see the sex of the baby. The baby was out. I was silently sobbing inside; I was not able to answer Ayesha.

'Doctor, let me sleep, leave me alone, don't stitch me up. Please, doctor, leave me,' she seemed to be saying to me.

She, on her part, was not getting enough courage to hear the verdict; she could sense her fate from my silence. I completed the stitches, gave her sedation, and left the labour room without congratulating her or blessing her on the forehead, as I do for every woman delivering after a painful, exhaustive labour.

My throat was choked. The miracle was not granted by God.

Fate Always Has Other Plans

I WAS rushing towards the OPD when I noticed a familiar face. An elderly woman, around 60, in a cotton sari was telling two young, chirpy twin girls, obviously her grandchildren to be careful as they swung their little brother between them. All three kids were laughing and giggling.

I recognised her immediately as well as the children. The girls had hazel eyes just like their father, who was in the army. It was a joy to see that the kids I had delivered had grown up so well and looked happy and healthy. The girls were now eight, and their brother was four.

They brought back memories of their birth. The girls were born prematurely via Caesarean section. The couple had consulted me for difficulty in conception due to the husband's irregular presence because of his army duties. I had prescribed ovulation induction medication, which could result in a twin pregnancy, but they were fine with it. She had conceived that same month.

After a few months, her husband was called away on duty, leaving her with his mother. As with many traditional mother-in-law-daughter-in-law relationships, she was made to perform all household chores despite her growing belly. One day, during her 32nd week, her water broke. I had to perform a Caesarean section because the mouth of the uterus was closed, and amniotic fluid was leaking profusely. She delivered twin girls, each weighing just over a kilogram.

I called an ambulance to shift them to the NICU, but her mother-in-law intervened. 'We can't afford expensive care for girls,' she said. 'If God is with them, they'll be fine; otherwise, it's His will.'

I argued that if her son, the girls' father, were here, he would have insisted that they go to the NICU for necessary care. But she insisted, 'He's not here, doctor. It's my decision, and we don't have money.'

I couldn't do much other than spend the whole night providing oxygen support with a mask and an Ambu bag. The nurse fed them neonatal formula throughout the night. By morning, the girls were pink and crying healthily. I was exhausted, but happy. After handing the babies over to their mother, I left for the day, praying that the brave girls would grow up healthy.

They never returned either for vaccinations or follow-ups. I assumed they went to a government or to an army hospital for those. Their baby brother was also born by my hands four years later, on the sixth day just after my own Caesarean section. I remember my house was full of guests celebrating my baby boy's birth. I was still feeling guilty and burdened by the thought of all I had personally undergone throughout to see the birth of my own son.

My phone had rung, and a voice said, 'Doctor, please

come for my delivery. I trust no one but you.' I had instantly recognised her voice. 'How are you? You're pregnant? Which hospital? I'll be there as soon as I can.'

It was the same nursing home, which was just five minutes away from my house. I sneaked out from the back door. She was in labor, when I reached, and her previous scar was thinned out, and she needed an urgent Caesarean section. Her husband was by her side. We shifted her to the OT and soon, their baby boy was born.

'How are the girls?' I asked the grandmother. 'They seem to be doing fine. Now they have their brother to protect them. Lucky girls.'

'I hope they're vaccinated, and please ensure the boy is vaccinated on schedule. Many congratulations to you,' I said before leaving.

Today, in the corridor of this expensive hospital, she was happily running after her grandson. She must be here for his vaccinations, I guessed. I tapped her on the shoulder. "Have you recognised me? Do you remember how I resuscitated these girls the day they were born? Look at them now, merrily swinging their brother between them."

She started crying on my shoulder, holding my hand. I was wondering if I had said something wrong. 'I'm sorry if I upset you. Why are you crying?'

'No, doctor, you didn't say anything wrong,' she sobbed. 'The boy can't walk. His legs are weak. That's why the girls are holding him, supporting him, one on either side. He has a musculoskeletal problem from birth.'

I was left speechless.

Sushmita and Shrija

'DOCTOR, I want a boy this time. We have a daughter and now we want a son,' the patient's husband said to me.

'She is pregnant, please do all the tests to ensure that the baby is all right,' said the man in his Telugu accent, while sitting in my OPD with his wife and a three-year-old daughter.

I wrote down antenatal investigations and advised her to take supplements. Her nuchal scan was due. He said he couldn't afford a pricey ultrasound centre, so I suggested an economical one.

On his next visit, he was on time and proudly informed me how he was taking good care of his wife, listing the names of all the fruits and dry fruits, *kesar, anjeer,* beetroot juice and many other nutritious things which he was feeding her. He also asked me what all she should not be doing, including carrying heavy weights, climbing stairs, and travelling by bus or auto.

We had a long consultation on her health and well-being during pregnancy. I advised him that double marker is mandatory after nuchal scan, so he should get this blood test done and meet me with the report in a day or two.

He hailed from the southern state of Andhra Pradesh which is supposedly full of orthodox families. In south India, Kerala has the maximum population of females. Male-female ratio is always in favour of females, which I felt, was natural. Hence, people there do not go for female foeticide or sex selection before birth. Whatever the gender is, if they want two kids and if they happen to be girls, they comply with it, and no hard steps are taken to correct the family's gender proportions. In my practice, I have seen this is the trend among my south Indian patients.

OPD on Saturdays is usually full of back-to-back appointments. Already running late, I slowly made my way through the crowd of patients waiting in the reception area.

The first patient entered with her husband and greeted, 'Hi, good evening doctor, how are you? A very happy new year to you.'

'I am good, yes, happy new year to you too. And how have you been?' I replied.

'Doctor, this lower back pain and pelvic pain has started bothering me. Twisting and turning on my bed also feels like a task now. Otherwise, I guess I'm good.'

'But doctor, she is not eating properly. Please advise on her diet. She is not eating fruits except for guava and banana. She doesn't seem to like an iron-rich diet. She hates spinach and beetroot. She is also unable to tolerate the smell of mutton and iron tablets give her constipation. She does not like paneer or eggs. What do we do, doctor,' her husband asked.

He was visibly anxious about her health.

'This is a problem. You have practically ruled out every nutritious food.'

'Ok, Sushmita, let me tell you, right now your baby must be weighing around 250-300 gm as you are in your fifth month. So as far as amount of diet is concerned, you are not supposed to have diet for two people. However, a healthy balanced diet is advised. Let me suggest you an alternative diet of protein and dry fruits. You can have all the pulses, boiled and sautéed, smoothies, fruits and dried fruits in custard or porridge.'

'Yes, this is good. I will try this.' The patient seemed happy and satisfied with the meal plan.

Deep within, I was counting the minutes spent with each patient and multiplying that number with the huge number of patients waiting outside, along with the waiting time for new walk-in patients. But from the exterior, I looked calm, composed, eager to answer any query or doubt. I smiled, replied graciously, and wished them well.

The second patient was Shrija, the pregnant woman hailing from Andhra Pradesh.

I got worried and thought to myself that he might take a lot of time, on account of his overtly concerned nature for his pregnant wife's diet. I asked them to sit.

'Doctor, we got the double marker test, and I am worried about the report. I googled it. I could not sleep at night. If this child has Down syndrome, we don't want to keep it. Down syndrome means a mentally retarded child, doesn't it, doctor?' her husband asked.

After a momentary pause, he continued.

'See doctor, I went through much trouble for this pregnancy. I went to a small village near Bellary for this, stayed there with family for ten days in a small room. I had to take leave from work. I told you we want a baby boy this time, we have a girl already, didn't I, doctor? So, this time we either have a boy or no baby at all. See doctor, you must understand, even if it does not matter to me, my mom wants a boy. I am her only son, doctor. Who will take care of my money, and who will take care of us later, doctor? I am a science graduate, I think logically, doctor. I calculate and analyse like you doctors do before planning treatment. Moreover, if we were back in the South, it was ok doctor, but we have been living here since many years now, along with my mom. Her thinking has changed as she saw all these North Indians craving for sons. I can't help it, doctor.'

I was listening silently, and wanted to explain to him that high risk did not mean absolute risk, it only meant that the possibility was high.

But I was enjoying the conversation and wondering how people try to justify their wrong beliefs and speak at length to justify their actions. He was trying to convince me, and suddenly I was not in a hurry to stop him or request him to wrap up fast as other patients were waiting. Instead, I was in a mood to hear him out. I had heard so many stories and explanations on this subject, but then every time there was something new that came my way, it would still surprise me.

Everyone wants a baby boy! No matter where they hail from!

He was in no mood to listen to me and was going on and on. He was not bothered about the long line of patients outside. He totally believed in his line of reasoning, and I had to play along. On the one hand, I was genuinely interested in all the possible stories of families craving for a boy. On the other hand, as doctors, we should not let patients feel that we are belittling their beliefs. His wife was in sync with him as if he was her spokesperson. She was smiling all through and was pleased to have him by her side.

He continued again, 'See doctor, there is a sadhu in Bellary who distributes medicine for having a baby boy. He does this service free of charge. But he distributes this medicine only on Thursdays and Sundays. Both days are mandatory to attend. Medicine should be taken as soon as you are sixty-eight days pregnant. If your calculations are wrong and you took it before the sixty-eighth day, it's not going to work. If it is a little too late, again the effect would wane away. I calculated it all doctor. We were right there on the said day. He prepares a powder from some herbs and then he makes a concoction from it. He makes the lady lie down on the couch, with her head dangling down. Then he applies a few drops of the concoction in the right nostril for a baby boy, and in the left nostril for a baby girl. But no one comes for that, you know, for there is not a single demand for a baby girl! The nasal application should be repeated the subsequent Sunday.'

I shuddered at the thought of someone putting some strange fluid down my nostril.

'It must have felt bad, right, Shrija? Awful taste! Poor you!'

She was smiling, and still grinning from ear to ear. 'No, no doctor, it was ok, no taste, smell or pain.'

'Doctor, there is more to it. After the second dose, he gives us one powder tasting like chalk, or calcium carbonate. We need to soak it overnight and let it settle in the water, and then take out the water which is clear and above the chalk. Then drink this the next Thursday to complete the course. One

more thing, the lady should not eat anything during these three days. Only milk, not boiled or sweetened, and boiled rice throughout the day,' Shrija's husband added.

I looked at the smiling Shrija, and wondered how she could tolerate all this.

'You had to undergo such a tough task!' I couldn't help but say at last.

'Yes doctor! That's why I wanted to confirm that the baby is perfect and healthy. I don't want a mentally retarded baby. Life is not worth it with that kind of baby. I am a busy man, and I don't want to have that trouble. Not at all.'

'Ok, it is quite a story. I understand your concerns and can feel your stress. Let's do a chorionic villus biopsy or amniocentesis to confirm it. You should visit me tomorrow. Let's fix an appointment with the foetal medicine specialist.'

'Ok doctor, thank you.'

'Will see you tomorrow, and till then, I will get proper information about the procedure,' added Shrija. She was smiling proudly on her way out.

My receptionist had peeped in twice during this consultation. The queue had grown, and the patients were getting restless.

A Gynaecologist is Every Girl's Best Friend

'HI DOCTOR,' a young girl with sharp features and a dusky complexion said as she entered my room. She seemed unable to contain her excitement.

'Doctor, I have come all the way from Kolkata. I have been searching for your address for long. I could not find your phone number anywhere on the internet. Then I found you on 'tacto' and booked this appointment. Doctor, I wish to seek your guidance.'

I was overwhelmed. This young woman had come all the way for my advice from Kolkata and had gone looking for me in an unfamiliar, unknown city, even staying in a hotel for a night just to visit me!

'Please take a seat. Relax. How did you get my reference? How can I be of help to you?'

She replied, 'Doctor I am a Central Government teacher. We had a training camp in Kolkata, where teachers and other government professionals had come from different states. It was a CRPF camp. During my training programme, I met a girl who was talking highly about you. You had delivered her

sister's baby. We discussed my periods problem as well and exchanged numbers. I couldn't find a good doctor in both Patna and Kolkata, so I asked her for your photo and contact details, and then, I came to you.'

She paused, and then continued. 'One of the doctors there told me that I will not be able to conceive ever. Please guide me.'

'Yes, please go ahead and walk me through your problem with your menstrual cycle,' I said to her.

'Doctor, I get very little bleeding every month, hardly one or two days and cycles are not regular. These are a few of my reports.'

She handed me her thyroid and prolactin values which seemed normal. Even her ultrasound report suggested a normal condition. I explained to her thoroughly all the possible causes of decreased menstrual flow and planned her investigations with respect to her menstrual cycle.

I suggested a series of tests to be done from day one to day four, such as TBPCR of menstrual blood, LH, FSH, AMH, DHEAS, Fasting and PP Insulin and HbA1c and pooled serum prolactin fasting sample and ultrasound.

'Please send all these reports via email and we will discuss it further on the phone,' I told her.

Her partner who was sitting quietly since the beginning, thanked me with moist eyes.

'Doctor, I had to take leave from my work. I had to leave a very important project in the middle to meet you. We have our flight booked for tomorrow morning. We were scared when the doctor there said that my wife won't be able to conceive ever or might not survive during the birthing process. Thank

you very much for taking up her case and working on her diagnosis. We will get back to you for further opinion with the test reports.'

Obstructed Labour

'I AM a very old patient of yours and wanted to meet you for my pregnancy check-up. You had operated upon me in the Healing Hospital about five years ago.'

From her file, the whole case was live in front of my eyes after so many years. The resident had called me to see a patient in obstructed labour, living in an adjacent village. The midwife had tried hard to deliver her vaginally, but the baby was stuck.

The patient was exhausted, dehydrated, drowsy and in terrible agony, her hand was on her vagina. She was crying in terrible pain and saying: 'It's tearing apart, my inside is tearing, my bones are shattering, let me die.'

The Bandl's ring was dividing her abdominal wall into two halves. The upper segment of her uterus was hard and bulging like a football agitated with constant beating under the effect of oxytocin, while the lower segment bulged like a balloon, stretched to its limit to receive the foetus. Both her upper and lower segment worked in tandem, as she contracted every time, and her foetus descended through her bony pelvic cavity (iliac bone, pubic symphysis, ischial bone, coccyx). It's a birth canal, and to enter it, there is one and only one prerequisite. The baby had to bow its head to the Almighty, bow till its chin touched the chest, the shortest diameter for the foetus to get accommodated inside the pelvic cavity. If the baby raised its head a little, and if it would be a little more upright, it would present its face, and won't be able to squeeze or mould through the bony pelvis.

Facial bones are fixed, not flexible like skull bones. Skull bones are like scales, overlapping on each other, to present the shortest diameter to enter (moulding). Once the head is inside the bony pelvic cavity, the jutting of spinous processes on both sides might obstruct the descent of the head, a challenging process, which requires moulding, squeezing, meandering, screwing, and rotating to make the baby descend in the outlet cavity. The manoeuvring of the head, neck, and shoulders continues till the crowning of the head at the perineum is followed by stretching the neck towards the spine. The baby faces the earth on coming out of the birth canal, eyes downwards, then turns sideways till shoulders slip out, and then, finally the body and legs come out.

But unfortunately, it didn't happen with this patient and her baby.

The foetus or the baby was stuck somewhere in the birth canal, and couldn't mould, squeeze, or rotate, due to extra-long spinous processes projecting inside the canal, or because of the very flat walls of the iliac bone, somewhat akin to a cone-shaped pelvis instead of a bowl-shaped one. The birthing process and the crowning of the baby's head isn't always smooth, and many conditions are to be fulfilled

by the mother-child duo. Not all mothers' birthing canals have a pelvis shaped like a wide bowl, roomy as a receptacle, supported with strong, healthy muscles.

So, the baby was stuck, unable to come down as its passage was obstructed in the bony canal. The mother struggled with strong contractions. The mother's body worked in full force, pushing the baby down with each contraction and the baby was transmitting the push through its body to its head, to make its appearance in the world. Unfortunately, there seemed to be a strong wall and bony nail blocking the baby's way. Eventually, the contractions dampened, and a natural, protective programme took over in the uterus. If the bony pelvis is not shaped right for vaginal birthing, contractions would stop to prevent rupture of the uterus. So, as a doctor, it's not hard to figure out what to do.

If contractions had been stopped by the body's instinct, there was evidently some disproportion between the baby's head and mom's pelvis, and therefore vaginal delivery would not be possible. This was the obvious conclusion.

I sometimes thought, all animals deliver vaginally. How is their birth never obstructed? Aren't we all animals first, standing on two hind legs? But our posture has narrowed our pelvises. Moreover, our lethargic lifestyle has seemingly weakened our bones and muscles. And yes, even animals have obstructed labour, occurring in minimal percentage, but this fact is hardly ever reported.

But when one ignores signs from nature, and we keep pumping drugs to increase contractions, encouraging the mom to push hard to expel the baby out, catastrophe results. The baby's head starts crushing the urinary bladder wall in front

and the rectal wall behind. The uterine walls are eroded. The baby's head keeps grinding through neighbouring structures, squashing the layers of the uterus which is caught between the baby pushing down and the blockade.

With this patient, the baby's head was compressed all around with pelvic bones. Under tremendous strain, the baby started collapsing, unable to get enough blood supply to its brain. The heart started beating fast to flush enough oxygen to the brain to fight a little longer, but after some time, the heart became tired, too. The foetal heartrate dropped.

The baby was stuck, the mother was tired, and the baby had pooped. I was trying to save a patient who was almost on her deathbed.

'Shift to the OT immediately, Catheterise Urinary Bladder,' I instructed.

I had delivered the freshly dead foetus, smeared in his own poop. I was in such pain, seeing the 3.8 kg baby, lying lifeless.

'Let's explore the surrounding structure,' I said to my team.

Uterine walls of the mother were thin and transparent, the urinary bladder was shredded, and urine was flowing inside the abdominal cavity. All the layers were mashed, difficult to identify and separate. There was continuous dribbling of urine through her vagina, and the stench of the urine filled her body causing constant wetness in the perineum and rashes on her thighs.

Vesico vaginal fistula, the condition the patient was suffering from is not rare in our country. Home deliveries, deliveries by untrained *dai*, quacks practising in remote villages, often result in ruptured uteruses, perforated intestines and torn urinary bladders.

But we needed to save this lady; her urine was draining through her vagina continuously like a tap left open. The posterior wall of her urinary bladder was torn. We repaired it meticulously, and checked it for watertight closure, catheterised with urethral catheter, and sutured her uterine walls after removing the placenta and clots. She would need four weeks catheterisation to recover from the condition. The surgery went well, thankfully, and we came out of the OT, satisfied.

The mother lost her firstborn to obstructed labour. The boy fought till his last breath. If she was taken up for Caesarean delivery early on, he would have been saved. She was the same patient in my OPD—pregnant again.

She was happy but scared in the same breath and terrified of the traumatic, horrifying experience of her last childbirth. She kept wondering if she would ever be able to hold a live baby of her own. During these nine months of gestation, anything bad could happen. What if her baby dies early, what if her body is not strong, what if again she had to undergo long unending agony post-delivery, and so on?

After reassuring her, we discussed the most important threat to this pregnancy—repercussions of the previous obstructed labour and repair of lower uterine segment and cervix. It was understandable that a normal vaginal delivery will not be attempted this time, but more than that, the challenge was to take the pregnancy to term. Chances of mid trimester abortion due to weak cervix (the mouth of uterus, which holds the pregnancy antigravity) were high. We would require a surgery around eleven weeks on the cervix to hold the pregnancy till term.

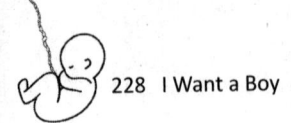

They had come from a faraway place, some small town where medical facilities were not good. The nearest hospital was forty minutes away. We decided the patient needed a visit around 11-12 weeks, for level 1 scan and stitch (Macdonald's stitch) surgery.

However, due to Covid, she got her scan in her hometown. The scan results were normal, the cervix was of good length, and the baby was growing well. Following the lockdown, one day, she had pain in her lower abdomen. The foetus was bulging out from the cervix according to the clinician in their town.

Complete bed rest and tocolysis (to reduce uterine contractions) started, but it was of no avail. At eighteen weeks, the live foetus was expelled due to her weak cervix, resulting from her previous mishap. She lost her chances of being a mother, all over again.

Funny Incidents

'BRILLIANT, DR Anu, you did a bloodless vaginal hysterectomy in forty minutes! I have never seen such a surgical feat,' my colleague said, appreciating my work.

I worked for three years in a Central Delhi Hospital, doing as many as forty to sixty deliveries in a span of twenty-four hours. The OT used to be full of three major gynae cases, about six or so minor elective cases in addition to emergency OT running parallel in full swing. The sheer number of cases per day would train any amateur surgeon well. But the scene in the OT was so confusing every day that you would wonder whether it was an OT table or a fish market.

Let's picture a regular day in the life of a government hospital's permanent doctor (a consultant or HOD). The morning tea and gossip for an hour is followed by ward rounds. Ward rounds doesn't mean visiting wards to see patients but sending summons to the resident doctor from Labour Room and wards to come with the list of patients and narrate the series of events from last evening. And evenings, when the consultants leave the hospital, they should be abreast with

every tiny detail of all serious incidents, severe morbidities like obstetric hysterectomy and maternal or foetal mortalities. It should seem as if they were aware and awake throughout the night, monitoring patients.

The exhausted resident would stand in front of the few senior consultants explaining every detail of each case. The consultant with the hot cup of tea in hands would analyse their actions. Why didn't you start that drug? What was the need for this procedure? Why was transverse incision given? It is so difficult to do repeat C-sections on transverse scar. You people will be gone after three years for us to suffer from your modern adventures, they would tell us.

Caesarean section to deliver the baby was done by giving a long vertical incision on the abdominal wall from the naval till the pubic bone in those days. Transverse incision was introduced long back for better post-operative recovery and a scar hidden below and behind your panty (also called bikini scar). However, government doctors wouldn't let anyone try newer techniques. What if new methods turned out to be fallacious? What if post-operative adhesions are severe, they would say.

For their own mental peace, they wouldn't let postgraduate students or resident doctors learn newer, well-accepted methods. As government employees, they had secured, fixed-hour jobs with no added responsibilities and they didn't want us to disturb their 'comfortable' lives. They were the ones who went home without tension at 4 pm when resident doctors handled the hospital efficiently, with diligence and intelligence. Consultants would go for shopping to nearby markets during hospital hours as well or would call vendors to their chamber.

No resident doctor would ever ask their help in handling the cases. We were more than sufficient and confident to handle every casualty with the help of our fellow colleagues. In all fairness, during daytime a few sincere consultants would come to help if there was a need, but a majority of them were not serious about their duties and about assisting us in the OT.

Senior consultants were only interested in gynae surgeries in the OT. They never let us do any of them. Abdominal or vaginal hysterectomy would be allotted to them in turns. Residents and postgraduate students would always assist them as second or third assistants. The surgeon on one side of the OT table, and the first assistant on the other side were the only people who could witness what was happening inside the abdominal cavity. Second or third assistants were not able to even look at the surgical site due to clustering. Their job was to hold the retractors to keep the intestines away from the operating area and keep pulling, almost till their shoulders would literally pain with the effort. If the operating surgeon was unable to do it properly, he would shout at these assistants to hold the retractor properly, or else to de-scrub.

However, to get selected as a second or third assistant was a privilege in those days, and it still is.

As resident or postgraduate students, we didn't learn any gynae surgeries, even when we were in Delhi's top medical institutes. Delhi's postgraduate gynae doctors are only obstetricians. Their gynae surgical skills are almost non-existent. In a vaginal hysterectomy or abdominal surgery, five doctors are scrubbed, which is hilarious, because only two are required. It takes 4-5 hours of laborious, back-breaking bending towards a small opening and even if one tries to participate in the steps of the surgery, one ends up learning nothing. This procedure should take no more than 45 minutes in experienced hands. Or maximum two hours, even if complexities surprise you in anatomical distortion.

I have often seen the surgeons struggling, fiddling, pulling or pushing, shouting at juniors for bad assistance and blaming them, requesting the anaesthetist for a little more relaxation of the muscles. And God forbid, if they accidentally slipped a bleeder or plucked a vessel with forceful suturing, the surgical scene would be drowned in a pool of blood, with the bleeder pumping blood in a pulsating motion. This happened once and I still remember it in vivid detail.

All hell broke loose that day, with hue and cry for mops, frantic calls to the general surgeon, immediate orders for the resident to de-scrub and run to get blood for transfusion. And instead of calmly suctioning the blood, while keeping a pressure on the bleeder and ligating it, we were asked to chant *Gayatri Mantra*. What utter nonsense!

The consultants seriously believed that the bleeding vessel was angry with us, and we needed to appease her by praying to God. The anaesthetist laughed, albeit with a serious expression on his face. We residents were really embarrassed with the moronic behaviour of our seniors. Suddenly, the general surgeon appeared like a saviour. All consultants looked towards him with pleading expressions, as if he was God-sent. The surgical resident who had been an intern in OBGYN just a while ago and was now posted in the general surgery department seized the moment to be a He-Man. He had barely learnt suturing of episiotomy after multiple attempts a few weeks earlier, but in GS, he had apparently become learned enough to manage a bleeding vessel in a major gynae surgery.

Surgeons make mockery of gynae doctors in government hospitals and that's why they send the junior most to respond to our calls. In fact, it is believed that the gynae consultants would have called for some petty bleeder or a small cut on the urinary bladder, which could be handled by even a first-year surgical resident. Our He-Man tackled the bleeding catastrophe in a jiffy and flew off, leaving all of us gynae doctors awestruck. We, the postgraduate students learnt that day that we should focus equally on what we rather should not do, to avoid disaster, than only concentrating on what we can do.

Thence, we were called glorified midwives, or *dai*, so to say—beautiful, feminine, overworked, moody and irritated young eligible doctors. This familiar image of gynae residents was in contrast with orthopaedic residents, who were called glorified carpenters. Their job was primarily to fix broken bones and joints with screws, hammers, saw and nails. Their knowledge of general medicine, on the other hand, was awfully poor. They were usually unable to examine a patient's ultrasound or ECG. These doctors were muscular and manly, and were naturally attracted towards fragile, helpless gynae doctors. Sometimes, gynae doctors, too, would be infatuated with their messiahs, 'the general surgeons'.

Safdarjung Hospital in Delhi was often made to function as an emergency room of AIIMS. Two of the busiest hospitals in Delhi stood across the road, often mirroring each other. Approximately ten thousand patients visited these hospitals every day. There was a continuous flow of sick, debilitated, crippled patients, dying from one morning till the next, with no respite. The duty doctors here had been transformed into human machines. They needed to act swiftly as soon as they joined as interns, the first clinical practice after finishing MBBS.

An intern is generally more learned in emergency medicine than any super specialist. Interns can perfectly start an IV line in a burnt patient, catheterise a tetanic opisthotonos patient, do lumber punctures in a newborn, draw blood from the femoral artery, puncture the neck to do tracheotomy, do venesection and still remain unassuming in their essential character. They are the foundations of the hospital system till date. The list of their essential duties is long and inexhaustible. It includes filling admission forms of patients, drawing blood samples for the lab, filling the forms for tests, entering admissions in the register, collecting reports from lab and x-ray department, entering examination notes to admission files, ordering medicines and entering doctor's orders into files, making discharge summaries, making sure birth certificate forms are filled post-delivery, making deliveries and marking MTP entries to the respective registers, arranging blood from blood bank, taking consent before surgery and so on.

Internship is their time to gain clinical knowledge. They enter the ward hesitantly like meek, innocent, pink lambs. I have seen the senior nurses reacting like butchers in front of them. They would frown at their group, and the new kids would be intimidated and rightfully so. The residents would be happy to see a fresh batch of helping hands. They would call them and teach them how to draw blood and many other techniques, to release their own burden.

I clearly remember one such incident.

'Doctor, please wear gloves… Come, let's learn how to insert cannula in this patient.'

The intern went to the nursing counter to fetch the gloves, and wore them with much difficulty, trying to slip the right fingers in each. And suddenly, a shrill shout startled him!

'Why are you wasting sterile gloves? You are supposed to wear these gloves, not the sterile ones. Already we are short of supply. We can't charge from the patients. Where do we get them if you people keep wasting stuff like this?'

The intern was perplexed.

This had been the start of our medicine practice, to be scolded by every Tom, Dick or Harry. Nurses would take sadistic pleasure teasing and tearing apart the junior doctors, but in all fairness, it were these very same nurses who also taught us the most. And if we would be obedient and respectful, they would be our teachers as well as our saviours.

The next day in the OT, one intern was asked to scrub with the resident. Other interns were also trying to figure out how to be useful in the OT. As soon as the intern wore the surgical gown, the echo from the other end broke him down.

'How can you waste a surgical gown? We don't have extra gowns for your luxury. These new doctors have no sense at all! They irritate me every year. I am done with them. Now I have one less gown for today's OT (operation theatre) list. Doctor, you should teach your interns to behave, shouldn't you?'

The intern was standing in the half-worn surgical gown, hanging limp on his shoulder, to be tied from the back. But who had the audacity to tie it now after realising the blunder? The other interns who were cursing themselves for not being selected to assist in the case were now sighing with relief that

they had escaped embarrassment. And the intern in the half-worn gown had stood dumbfounded, unable to understand the next step. We as interns were always clueless about the hospital's intricacies. We would be scolded, reprimanded till we became smarter! Initially it felt very humiliating, but eventually we realised that the anger was not towards us, but towards the faults in the system, itself, towards the scarcity of medicines, gloves, gowns, beds, and doctors. As soon as we absorbed ourselves in teamwork, as another moving wheel in the constantly running train of patient care, we started enjoying our duties.

We had often seen patients from the AIIMS emergency room being directed to Safdarjung Hospital, stating that it is an extension of AIIMS. It was seen as a big bone of contention between the two hospitals, shoving sick patients from one hospital to the other.

Being a doctor, handling emergency patients all the time, I know how hard it is to explain the condition of a very serious ICU patient to relatives. Sometimes they are aware of the gravity of the illness, but at other times, it doesn't sink into their consciousness. If a patient is on ventilator or life support, and is being pumped with oxygen, then to make his heart work and to extract urine from his kidneys is difficult—and they may not survive. We need to counsel the relatives daily and keep them posted about the severity of the patient's illness and chances of recovery. But even after explaining that most of the patient's organs have failed and machines are keeping him alive, the relatives still question: 'but are all other things, all right?'

'All other things? What other things,' I ask, surprised.

Heart, lungs, kidney and liver, the vital organs are failing, and are supported on machines. Then, which other things are we talking about?

It is always impossible to make them see any kind of sense.

Infertility (Male Factor)

I WAS getting late for the OT. The walk-in patients in the OPD were unexpected and out of turn most of the times. Though we try to plan OPD and OT according to the booked appointments, emergency or walk-in patients mostly upset the whole schedule.

I rushed towards the OT for a minor surgery, as the patient was already under anaesthesia. There had been repeated calls from the OT-in-charge to start the case. Suddenly, this patient whom I had seen a minute ago walked towards me with some query. I kept walking in the corridor and indicated to her that she should walk along with me and talk on the way. But she was crying silently, under her mask.

I looked at her eyes and said, 'Please come inside the OPD chambers.'

I took an about turn. We sat again, even while another patient was under anaesthesia, waiting for me to begin an operation.

'Are you crying?' I asked.

She started sobbing louder when I said this. I offered the

tissue paper, placed my hand on her shoulder and she kept quiet.

'Doctor, I was not clear about these instructions, please explain them to me again,' she said.

'Yes, I will, but first tell me why are you so worked up, and why are you crying? What exactly is bothering you?'

'Doctor, I think I am tired of fertility treatment. It's been eight years of our marriage. I have been to dozens of doctors, spending thousands of rupees on endless number of tests, ultrasounds and so on. Just because I am in a government job, I could afford it all. If I were in a private job, they would have thrown me out. The fallopian tube test was such a horrifying experience. No one had ever given me any hint of the tremendous pain it would cause me. I withstood that too. But I don't understand where exactly the problem is! You have no idea about the number of daily injections, the daily visits to all kinds of doctors, including allopathy, ayurvedic doctors I have done. I have also visited several temples; I have visited mosques. You have also seen all my reports. Even according to you there is no problem with me. Then why am I not getting pregnant yet?

'Everyone is asking me to continue with the treatment, observe fasts and try different dusts from the Moulavi. No one is questioning my husband. He has not undergone a single test, not even semen analysis. He believes that nothing could be wrong with him. Every time I go to him during my fertile days, he frowns. He simply refuses to have sex even on those three fertile days. If pregnancy was not in question, he wouldn't come near me ever. We don't have a sex life; so many times, I have begged him to have sex because I had taken multiple injections and was following ovulation with daily ultrasound monitoring. Doctors are frustrated because we would waste good eggs by not having intercourse. That's why they suggested IUI. But he was travelling for work every time. I wouldn't have wanted a baby so desperately, but the social pressure is too much for me to bear, doctor. I have not been able to focus on anything, neither on my job nor on myself. Most of the time I am irritated or unbearably sad. And again, I am here for another cycle of treatment with you. I am not sure if I want this or not. I can't think clearly regarding how to move forward. What is the way out?'

She was in pain while narrating her story and all I could do was to listen silently.

I was absorbing the pain of this woman. There were multiple problems, but they weren't anything new. The clinical problems could be dealt with. But the psychological part of it was more disturbing. The husband might be going through performance anxiety or experiencing some other pathology with libido or erection. Men are generally not forthcoming with their concerns. They just accept the abnormality and try to live with it. They mostly don't share this, even with their spouse.

Nonetheless, a remedy to this had to be found. Her hands in mine, we sat across each other till her tears had dried. She was much calmer when we walked towards the OT together. She said goodbye with the promise to come back the next month to discuss IVF.

Every patient is important to us, and our lives revolve around their concerns. The one in the OT and another one in the OPD were afflicted with different problems, but they were both in pain.

Their pain touched my very core. It is not only the symptoms or diseases they are suffering from, but it is the psychology around the diseases, the expectations of the family, the financial concerns that are also equally important; and we must weave a tailor-made medical plan for each of them.

Post-Delivery Blues

'PLEASE CALL my mom now.'

'Yes darling, calling everyone. You did it! You did it! Look at her, our little doll. How tiny she is. Oh my God, she has tiny hands and feet.'

'Doctor, why is she crying?'

'Babies cry to breathe. It's good for them. The first cry expands their lungs, don't worry. She is pink and active. If you want to take a picture, please click without the flash.'

'Yes, yes, sure doctor.'

Just then, the phone started ringing.

'Yes mom, you are a 'Dadi' now. A beautiful daughter is born, yes, through normal delivery. Please come, I am disconnecting your call as many are calling to wish.'

By evening, when I visited the patient in her room, it was full of relatives, sweets, laughter and love all around. The whole family was gathered, claiming their right on the baby. They wanted to hold the baby, play with her, and were calling out to her using several endearing names. The parents of the baby were sidelined. The mother was lying, exhausted from all her labour pains, half sleepy, smiling, happy to see her baby getting all the love and attention. The father's heart was filled with relief, surrounded with the love and support of his family.

A week later in OPD, she entered with a tired, fatigued look, wrapped in a shawl from head to waist, with a sad expression on her face.

'How are you? You look tired. It must be exhausting to be up all night to feed the baby. How are you coping with it all,' I asked her.

And she started crying. Her husband sat alongside in a chair, with a helpless expression on his face.

'Doctor, our baby got jaundice,' she said, sobbing.

'That's ok, it must be physiological jaundice, it's a very common occurrence. Sun bath or phototherapy usually corrects it. You shouldn't be so troubled by this,' I said reassuringly.

'Doctor, she was admitted in the hospital and till yesterday, we were very worried. Everybody at home said it was my turmeric consumption that caused her yellow skin. I have stopped eating chapati, rice, curd, turmeric, and many other things which might have caused her illness. I have restricted myself to one room, without TV, phone, or anything. I am going crazy, sitting all day, feeding her and cleaning poop, changing clothes 24*7. My neck, shoulder, and back are all aching. Still whenever my baby is crying, I am being blamed for her loose stool or tummy ache or gaseous pain.

'It is overwhelming to take responsibility for her sufferings when all I want to do is to protect her and provide the best care as much as I can. Sometimes I don't feel like feeding her. I just don't want to do anything. I am crying for no reason.

I feel guilty of becoming a bad mother. People blame me for not having enough milk supply, one of the reasons for her constant howling.

'And yes, the milk doesn't come in good flow even upon squeezing. My mother-in-law was recalling her breast being full and leaky all the time. It doesn't happen to me. She doesn't sleep for more than 10-15 minutes because of less milk supply. It seems she is perpetually hungry.'

'Dear, relax,' I told her.

'Have you ever wondered why kittens, pups and many other mammals do not require formula feed? Because they feed their newborns 24*7, till they develop enough stamina to extract enough. Sucking stimulates the brain glands to secrete prolactin and oxytocin hormones for breast milk to be let down and offer continuous milk supply. It is stimulated with the sight of the baby, by the baby's cry, and suckling.

'The greater the number of hours the baby suckles initially, the better the milk flow and supply. However, if we choose formula feed thinking the baby needs sleep or a pacifier, it decreases the feedback signals to the brain to eventually decrease the supply. The more the baby suckles, the stronger and constant is the signal, secreting regular milk supply and vice versa. Your newborn is developing stamina. It would sleep after a few suckles, then again swallow after a few suckles, then pause again. But sometimes, baby will sleep in your warmth near your musical heartbeat. Wake her up then, and remind her to finish her meal.

'Breastfeeding is guided by the baby, extracted by it laboriously. Till the baby develops good strength and stamina, it would seem to the mother that she is doing only one job all through the day—of nursing. In a couple of months, things would be better for feeding schedules and better sleep patterns. Your eating habits have no bearing on your baby's discomfort. All newborns take air while searching for the nipple or while suckling, and this is called aerophagia. That wind troubles them and it feels like a tummy ache is bothering them. All babies release gas by farting or burping and it has no correlation to the mom's dietary habits. So, honey, relax. We need a happy mom, not a perfect and sad mom.

'Let's discuss the role of ghee and jaggery, both being parts of a staple diet for a breastfeeding mom. Let's talk about its role in women, post-delivery and its modern alternatives,' I told her.

Ghee was fortified with Vitamin A and D in early post-Independent India, and it was advised by all to offer 5-7 kgs of ghee to a woman post-delivery to strengthen her bones. It was also good in preventing osteoporosis in her and rickets in the newborn. The Vitamin A supplement helps prevent night blindness in kids as well as in breastfeeding mothers. From 1950s till now, our grannies and moms were forced to eat kilos of ghee to strengthen their bones and eyesight. Since then, there has been this tradition of stuffing the pregnant woman with desi ghee in India. If they have gained 15-20 kgs in pregnancy, ghee would add another 20 kgs post-delivery. Breastfeeding moms are made to believe that ghee and jaggery are good for them and their newborns. Jaggery is added to buttery meals to increase their haemoglobin.

These days, doctors are prescribing iron, calcium, multivitamins, and Vitamin D during pregnancy and post-delivery. Thence, it is not required for all mothers to have ghee

and unnecessarily increase their volume and circumference.

The overwhelmed new mother and her caregivers had now understood the science behind breastfeeding and the importance of nutrition for the new mom. I hoped postpartum conflicts between the older generation and the naïve, yet scientific younger generation would be eventually resolved.

We need to counsel mothers and mothers-in-law antenatally and post-delivery to bring both generations on the same page. Post-delivery psychological support by a clinical counsellor should be mandatory. Cases of post-delivery blues and depression are on the rise. New mothers are not ready for a round-the-clock motherhood job. The life before baby and after baby is unimaginably different.

Mental preparation should start from the last trimester of pregnancy and counselling sessions must include the supporting family members as well.

Father-in-Law as a Sperm Donor

TWO MIDDLE-aged women entered my chambers. One was my old patient's mother-in-law, and the other was her sister.

'My sister is in lot of trouble, please help her, doctor. Her daughter-in-law is not able to conceive, even after two years of marriage.'

'Let's meet the patient first and her husband. Let me get all the information regarding their medical and personal history, and a few tests to ascertain their fertility status. Let's call them inside.'

'Doctor, let me explain it to you first, I am in a miserable state,' the mother-in-law said, shedding what seemed like artificial tears. She held my hands. 'Only you can save me, doctor. I need my grandchild, girl or boy doesn't matter. I will send my daughter-in-law first, please examine her and let me know if all is ok.'

The daughter-in-law came in, a young girl, barely nineteen years old, wearing a saree, covering her head, eyes down. Her menstrual cycles were regular, and she had no significant past

medical history. Her parents were also hale and hearty. By her medical history and general examination, she should have no issues with her fertility. I explained it to her mother-in-law and asked for a few test reports when she visited for her next consultation.

The mother-in-law asked her daughter-in-law to go out and wait in the reception lounge. Waiting for her to close the door, she turned towards me, and asked, 'So is she good, fertile?'

'I believe, yes. Her menstrual cycles are good. And she is in her best reproductive years. Still, let's wait for the reports. But it is equally required to test the husband. A simple test called semen analysis will tell us the fertile status of the husband's sperms. If your son is uncomfortable meeting a female clinician, I can refer him to a male urologist. It's totally understandable. However, test his semen quality first with this simple test.'

'You would like me to call him inside,' she asked.

'Yes, let's talk to him as well.'

In our conservative society, boys in their early twenties are often married off to beautiful, young girls. They are still studying themselves, and have no idea what the future holds for them. They are jobless and pampered, and dependent on their parents for their daily allowance. Because they themselves are treated as kids, no responsibility is expected from them. At such an age, they get married and enjoy the wife's company during the nights. During the day, the new bride is expected to do the household chores, carrying out the mother-in-law's orders like a robot without any intimacy being shown towards her. She cannot even take food by herself until her mother-in-law asks her to do so. She cannot do anything of her own accord without permission. She is not expected to rest or sleep till her mother-in-law allows her to do so. She cannot talk or sit with her husband during the daytime. After cleaning up the kitchen, and completing any other domestic duty left for the day, she would have to ask her mother-in-law if she was allowed to go to her room, where her husband would be waiting.

Here is the young man, her husband, who has been attending college and roaming around with his friends all day and is now waiting for his wife, while she is exhausted physically, lost in an unloved, uncaring world of strangers in which she is expected to satisfy her husband's desires. She too is just a young girl who wants to watch TV, talk to friends, play games on her phone, or enjoy some hobby. But who cares! That is unimaginable, for once she is married, her duties are to take care of her new house and its residents. A bonded labourer 24x7, she is also expected to carry forward their genetic lineage, preferably deliver a male baby and carry on with the same routine for the rest of her life.

As expected, the young man who walked in was a shy young fellow whose hair was oiled and parted sideways. He entered with his head bent and hands folded as he greeted me. His mom asked him to sit down. His left side was paraparetic, and he was holding his left hand with his right, supporting it from hanging loose. His left leg was weak and lagged behind him as he walked. His facial features suggested he was mentally challenged. I noticed that he himself was not answering my questions, but his mother was. He couldn't comprehend what I was asking him. His mother, after displaying her son to me, asked him to go outside to join his father. The boy obeyed.

'Doctor, now you have seen him. He is of low intelligence since birth. Doctor said his brain was swollen; a shunt is placed in his brain since birth. He is my only son, born after three daughters. I have been struggling to rear him. My whole youth has been spent cleaning up his poop and pee. Till date, he has not learnt to control his bowel movements or urine. I have never been to family functions or holidays because of him. I love him so much as he is our only son, but now I am tired. I am getting old; my stamina is waning. My strength is wasted.

'Who will look after him once we are gone? That's why I wanted him to have a partner, who can take care of him. She is a nice girl from a very poor family. She is very lucky to have found us as a family. Right now, she is good, happy with all the luxuries of life, but God knows till when. I want her to belong to us with a blood bond, her own child from my son. That way, she will never leave him. No mother will run away, leaving her child behind. And as you have seen now, my son is incapable of sex or even masturbation. We have got his testicular biopsy too. Even that is hopeless. He doesn't have sperms. Prolonged treatment must have killed his ability to make sperms. So, we would want to go for IVF with donor sperms.'

It was as if my brain was getting roasted on a low flame. Wasn't this the height of selfishness and insensitivity? What if this young girl in front of her was her own daughter? Would she behave the same way? Was it right to impregnate a young girl and tie her to a mentally challenged person? Is this right?

But keeping my cool, I kept listening. I was convincing my mind to not speak so as not to hurt a mom's feelings. I was training my brain that in this strange world, we must keep an open vision and accept strange solutions. I was swallowing my words, absorbing their situation, and trying to figure out a management plan as soon as it was needed.

'So, you want an IVF pregnancy with donor sperm? That is possible. Let's wait for her next periods and put her on injections for egg formation. As soon as we retrieve her eggs, you select a sperm donor, and we are good to go,' I said.

'Thanks a lot, doctor, so it is possible! We will always be thankful to you.' And she kept on wishing me luck and fame and success. She was so relieved.

But the blow was yet to be received. She wanted her husband (or girl's father-in-law to donate his sperm and be the donor). That was the only way to ensure their genetic lineage, else it will only be her baby, and not linked to their family at all. And in that case, it was possible for her to leave their son and seek a better life in the future, somewhere else. That's why they wanted the boy's father to be the father of the boy's child. This was confusing, utterly wrong, and outrageous, as well as illegal. They also had planned that the daughter-in-law should be kept in the dark regarding the source of the sperm. She should think that the child is her husband's, and from their wedlock, the mother-in-law told us. This belief would keep her rooted to their lives, and they would be able to enjoy a healthy grandson, and have an heir to the ancestral property.

I let out an obstructed sigh; my brain was about to blast. Thank God, my expression of disgust was masked. With a very calm demeanour, I refused their requests. I refused it all—their request of keeping the patient in the dark, request to make grandfather the donor, and request to carry out the case.

As a final blow, the last request was to select a male embryo for IVF pregnancy.

'Gender selection before embryo transfer is illegal and unethical here,' I said sternly. 'I will leave you with your thoughts to decide what is right or wrong!'

My Bhasmasur Act During Covid

IN HINDU mythology, there is a character devoted to God and his work, but he has this desire to rule the world till eternity. He wanted to be immortal. He followed strict prayers, invoking Lord Shiva for months together. Lord Shiva, the ever-generous, benevolent God, appeared before him and enquired what he wished for. Upon hearing that he sought immortality from Shiva, the Lord hesitated, but Bhasmasur was adamant. He accused Shiva of being unfair. After giving a lot of thought and with confusion brimming within Him, Lord Shiva granted Bhasmasur his wish to be immortal, but on one condition. The condition was that if he ever placed his hands on anything, whatever he touched would instantly turn into ashes.

Ironically, the minute his wish was fulfilled, he tried to touch Lord Shiva, and was about to turn Him to ashes. Gods feared him from that day, and the boon he was armed with. He had every God in heaven running from him trying to save themselves. At this point, the seniormost God, Lord Vishnu, who was known for his very prudent solutions, presented himself to the invincible Bhasmasur in the disguise of a beautiful dancer, an *apsara*. Bhasmasur instantly fell for her and wanted to marry her. She proclaimed she had a condition; the person whom she would marry should match her perfection in dance. Bhasmasur pleaded to the *apsara* to teach him how to dance, and not reject him outright.

As he started learning to dance under her intoxicating influence, his guarded movements slowly became more open and started to flow beautifully. He was enjoying every minute with the dancer, feasting his eyes on her flexibility, her expressions, her majestic beauty, the rhythm of her gracious movements. He was hypnotised in her spell, and was ecstatic in love. In the rhythm of the dance, they spun together, with arms outstretched, and soon, she led him to clasp his hands right over his head. In this ecstatic state of dancing, he vanished in smoke, charred to ashes.

In reading this story, I found an interesting parallel to my own journey of life, which is why I chose to start my narrative here by describing the plight of Bhasmasur.

I was writing my medical entrance exams for Wardha Medical College, an extremely prestigious college. The exam questions were easy, and my parents were waiting in the scorching heat outside besides their scooter. I revised my answers and was satisfied. I had to write a paragraph on Mahatma Gandhi, his ideology and anything about his life. This college, I knew, believed in Gandhian values, which I was against, personally. I refused to write anything good in that space even when I was aware that my good score would have no relevance if this question was not answered.

Against all odds, I believed that they would consider my

overall score, or performance much more than an answer based on Gandhian ideology. How naïve and foolish was I. How would it matter if I had written a few false lines? Believing in something might be ideal, but pretending to do something else is the clever and more practical solution. But my conscience was so strong, that it stopped me from being logical.

But of course, I never got a call from Wardha Medical College, though I had tried being argumentative and my father heard me at a point when I was fighting with my own mind about the best way forward–and whether to follow the ideology or rule set by others or not. He must have thought that she must learn through her own experience. He might have believed that one exam did matter, but it was not enough to break my belief system.

Ironically, I am following the same Bhasmasur act even today again when I am on the wrong side of forty! It has been thirty years from the time when I gave my medical entrance exam. Have I really learnt my lesson after so many years?

Since the corona virus entered our lives, the media has been spreading fear. While in reality, it might just be a mild, upper respiratory tract infection, self-limiting in 95 per cent cases, but still we panicked.

The mass mentality was this: 'Save yourself from others, as everyone is a possible carrier of this virus. And if someone gets the virus, avoid being in the vicinity of that person, stigmatise the person and his or her family, stop talking to them or even calling them over the phone. A Covid-positive individual, though healthy and showing no symptoms, was suddenly socially boycotted. The person was isolated, not allowed to talk to his or her family members, or even allowed to touch or

hug them. People started blaming that person for not taking enough measures to protect himself and for breaching the conduct of prevention. If by chance, one got infected again, twice with symptoms or no symptoms but with a positive Covid report, the mental trauma inflicted by society was unbearable.

A breach in precautionary steps for the second time was unpardonable.

When the first wave of Covid was announced in the country, preventive protocols and guidelines were circulated—covering head with surgical cap, wearing PPE gowns, gloves, shoe covers, and face shields. Everyone was walking in an astronaut's suit. The virus was said to be in the air, on every surface. Many doctors stopped seeing patients altogether. Many others bought special masks with filters in them. Those masks cost somewhere between ₹25,000 to ₹1 lakh.

Patients with upper respiratory tract infection were not allowed inside the hospital building. They were seen by the physician in makeshift chambers outside. Covid test was mandatory for all patients. Before admission for delivery or any other surgery, both patient and attendant needed a negative report. Emergency admissions were taken in the Covid ward, equipped with nurses and doctors with PPE kits. The arrangements were well in place and were followed strictly to prevent the spread of the disease.

However, for a doctor it was nearly impossible to be in full PPE all the time. Masks had become a part of our skin or should I say it started to look like an undergarment, and after a point, removing it in public felt almost vulgar! Families couldn't bear the thought of contracting Covid. Because of

their fear, they stayed indoors, and never allowed even maids or vendors to enter their premises.

However, all these precautions didn't help, because ultimately, most people eventually did contract the virus in some way or the other. And when they did, they broke down, cried, and realised that like lepers they could spread this deadly virus to others.

In the hospital, a mother wouldn't touch her new-born after delivering to protect it from her infection. The newborn was often alone in NICU, and no parent was allowed till they tested negative. Grandparents couldn't come as they were living far away in locked down cities. Neighbours were scared to help because of one's positive Covid status. I encountered such situations many a times.

We tried to counsel the newly delivered mother and psychologically distressed father. So, I was once caught consoling a Covid positive patient's husband. Many a times after taking out my PPE before leaving the hospital, I would be greeted by patients visiting the hospital for reasons other than pregnancy. They would be stopped from entering and we would be forced to see their reports in the corridors. We were in masks all the time to protect one another. But if that patient turned out to be positive, then I too was stopped from coming to the hospital till I got my Covid test after five days and it turned out to be negative.

The argument here was why was I caught talking to a potential positive patient on CCTV without PPE? I was blamed for not taking the guidelines seriously. After removing PPE, I wasn't supposed to be near any patient. The argument with the management that was governed by MBA graduates

was that a mask was enough to protect me proved futile. I was to be blamed, removed from my post, and from duty. I was reduced to nothing. I suddenly became a non-entity.

As a doctor, my professional life came to a halt and my patients were informed about my quarantine and told that they wouldn't be treated by me till my report proclaimed me as Covid negative. My doctor friends started blaming me for not following the norms, and my family was angry at my irresponsible behaviour at the cost of my life earnings, my position, and reputation. It felt as if years of my medical practise were in jeopardy.

The truth was nothing would have happened if the N95 mask was in place. Moreover, I hadn't even examined the patient, as it was only an act of counselling. Was I like Bhasmasur in this situation? Knowingly, I broke the Covid guidelines. My colleagues could not support me on this, because these were government policies and protocols that were perfectly moulded by bureaucrats and corporate heads with the objective to expel someone or deduct one's salary.

The first wave was difficult because authorities were trying to control the spread of the virus through stringent actions. Labelling houses as Covid positive and barricading them created quite a scare in society. People were traumatised more with the societal boycott than with the cough or fever they had contracted.

In the hospital, we were facing the brunt of strict Covid rules. We were subjected to long hours of nonstop duties, fixed meal hours and regular Covid testing. The patient load was so much that the medical staff couldn't have a single meal on time. And authorities wouldn't allow meals to be served in

the duty room as per Covid protocol.

Although patient's food was served in rooms, but we couldn't have it there. Our request to serve food to the nurses who were on 48 hours duty was rejected outright. Either they come down to lunch halls or forgo their food. Some days even for water, we had to put up a fight. Other days. I would cook food for them and bring it to the hospital. Nurses complained as they were starved, and yet they kept healing patients. I fought for them with the authorities. But rules are rules.

Getting infected was sinful. Instead of empathy, patients as well as infected doctors were stigmatised. I was caught many a times with positive patients while I was either comforting or treating them. I somehow never contracted the infection, and I was never afraid of Covid either. The truth was that around 90 per cent infected people would get mild cough and fever and that's why I wasn't worried. I tried to inject the same logic into everyone around. But I was alone in my attempt and in my firm belief, that covering the face and mouth was enough along with hand sanitation.

After all, according to many, rules should be followed by one and all in every situation without any empathy shown towards Covid positive patients. People are usually cautious of being caught on the wrong side of the rule book.

My downfall was inevitable the minute I started questioning their authoritarian rules, asserting the basic rights of nurses as well as my own, asking for decent hours of work instead of putting in insane hours of duty and questioning the stringent rules, the lack of leaves, and threats of expulsion in times when people were losing their jobs.

Many rules were enforced. For example, a doctor or any

paramedic or nursing staff was not allowed to speak to patients without PPE, or even comfort them in corridors without protection, as stringent action would be taken if they did so. One weak moment of yours was what they were waiting for. This was an offence to the community, they would say.

One was blamed for trying to spread the disease because one did not follow PPE protocols. Nothing would work in your defence here. The people you were fighting for would also start to distance themselves from you. It was my foolishness that on many occasions, I had put my patients first. I was worried about their mental well-being and I thought that a comforting pat on the shoulder wouldn't harm. I wanted to convey to them that it's ok, that you are not a untouchable like some leper. Meanwhile, the news of the virus taking numerous lives was spreading online, in news channels in every country, in every nook and corner of the globe. We wanted to believe that things would be fine and that nothing bad would happen, but can one be hundred per cent sure?

The news of doctors dying with corona was overwhelming us and the medical fraternity.

Bhasmasur was still inside me, in the form of my rigid beliefs, and I had to kill him. You cannot live with your ideology if it's not in sync with the set norms. Wasn't this why Gandhi was assassinated? His ideologies were not synchronised with the masses. I shouldn't disappear like him, playing my own discordant and disturbing beats, completely out of sync with others.

I have read several books with one observation in common, *1984* by George Orwell, *The Kite Runner* by Khaled Hosseini, and many on Hitler, the tyrant, among others. The oppressor

never believed in his own ideology and lived completely differently to what he preached. But the disciplines he wanted people to follow were difficult, stringent to the extent that a breach was inevitable, and would result in cruel, inhuman punishment.

It was necessary to spread the scare, to thrust authority, and to rule over the ordinary. Taliban families lived an extravagant life in the West, where their women wore short dresses, drove cars, partied, and enjoyed an all-American lifestyle, but back in their own country, their men ruled over them in a barbarous and dictatorial way. According to Khaled Hosseini's books, women were pelted in front of crowds if they were seen walking alone on the open streets, or if caught looking at any man, or if they were not covered from head to toe.

George Orwell mentioned in his book that the authorities robbed the necessities from the common man and always encroached into their private lives. Any deviation from their definition of 'normal life' resulted in brutal torture. However, despite this oppression which the common masses were subjected to, the people in the government lived a lavish, normal life. Rules were to be followed strictly by the masses and they were meant to bring everyone in line, to whip them and keep them under control.

Let's draw a parallel here. Every doctor, for that matter, needed to be in one PPE protection kit to prevent the spread of Covid. In that case, it should also have been followed by the hospital authorities, nurses, and doctors. However, management people made their own rules about disease control without taking any inputs from doctors! By forcefully implementing rules, they reduced doctors to machines.

Doctors who were running the show on the frontline, meeting patients, treating them, comforting them, working day and night to put salaries into the administrative authority's accounts were flogged to bring in more patients. Their self-esteem got crushed and was ripped off at every turn, as they were reprimanded over any breach in observing precautions. Sometimes, administrators themselves were lax, but it could not be tolerated if doctors behaved like them. They treated doctors like mere educated human resources.

The system tames them, nails them, and milks them.

As I mentioned before, I was caught plenty of times sometimes just for comforting patients. Imagine breaking grave news to a patient from behind a plastic curtain and seeing them falling to the ground crying with fear. I would rather be on the wrong side of the rules than witness a human in pain and not offer a hand to help them pull out of it. I followed my own Bhasmasur act religiously, whether I was or not within CCTV surveillance.

I was quarantined many times for being near a positive patient, but even then, I made sure that I engaged with my patients online offering medical advice.

Healing others is my passion. I will pass through this life but once, and so, if there is any kindness I can show to my fellow beings, let me do it now and not deter or neglect it, as I shall not pass this way again.

Twisted Tale
A Funny Covid Story

LIFE IS not always full of sad stories. I can recollect a rather different case that happened during the same Covid years. A patient was creating ruckus outside my OPD chamber, which prompted me to get up and peek outside. An obese, dusky lady with a pregnant belly weighing almost 130 kgs was wanting to see me out of turn! She appeared very authoritative and was claiming to be my cousin.

I couldn't place her anywhere on my family tree, however, hard I tried. Before I could intervene, and rush back to my room which I so much wanted to in that moment, she grabbed me in the corridor and started talking in a rush.

'It's so good to see you. It took me so much time to reach you. You look so divine, better than the description given to me. I was not able to get your appointment. I wanted to be under your care through my pregnancy, but I could never get a slot. Now I am here to be delivered by you at last. I am your sister's friend, Meenu, who lives in MYZ Apartments. We are neighbours,' she said.

Now I remembered. My sister had messaged me that her neighbour who was also a believer of our Guru ji will come to consult me. The text was two days old. I had assured her that I would see her.

'Please wait, I will see you as soon as I am free. Please have a seat,' I told her.

She settled down for a while. But I needed to see her quickly because my sister had sent her and because she was creating a nuisance in the OPD area. So, we sat in front of each other. She had lots to say about her nine months' journey with many doctors. She had changed doctors frequently.

According to her explanation, one was not learned enough, the other less experienced, the third one was not compassionate and fourth was good in every measure, but then she got my sister and her reference. So, she was finally with the most intelligent, experienced, empathetic and beautiful doctor! She flattered me. I was listening. We flipped through her medical history, page by page. She was hypertensive, diabetic, overweight with term pregnancy.

Her astrologer had requested delivery time to be 12.30 midnight as *shubh muhurat* (auspicious timing). She wanted a favour from me that I show it as an emergency and not charge extra for the *muhurat*.

After a lot of discussion and review, the OT was booked for midnight the next day. This was during the time of the first Covid wave. We were supposed to wear face shield with masks, head covers and plastic gown in the OPD. And if caught on camera wearing even one item less than required, we were sent back home as per quarantine protocols.

In the evening, the list of all positive cases would be taken

out and the security team along with the medical superintendent and floor attendant would scrutinise video footage and if anyone was caught near the vicinity of a positive Covid patient he was told politely to stay at home for seven days.

On the evening of the *muhurat* case, I got a call from the superintendent of the hospital that I had been caught without a face shield in the corridor talking to a patient who had turned out to be Covid positive.

'That's bad,' I said, 'but I have a booked OT for tonight. Let me do the case with all the precautions and PPE kit.'

'No doctor, it won't be possible. It is for everyone's safety. We can't break the protocols.'

Despite my insistence, he didn't budge from his decision. I didn't know what to do. My patient was a very high-risk case, 130 kg morbid obesity with high blood pressure and diabetes. How to convey to the patient that I won't be able to do her Caesarean section delivery? Would she understand?

I messaged her stating the quarantine rules and my contact history with a Covid positive patient and reassured her that my colleague would take care of her case with good care.

Somehow, she didn't see the message till she got admitted at 10 pm. She was understandably enraged and threw abusive swear words to the staff and to the doctor on duty. She called the police and filed a case against me and the hospital for denying her optimum care. She messaged me something foul and even threw shoes at the cardiologist and anaesthetist, who visited her in the room before her surgery. After many apologetic attempts and explanations, which she wouldn't accept, I had to eventually block her number.

But on that fateful night, the police came, registered an

FIR, and requested her to go home if she didn't feel comfortable in our hospital. She shouted some more, cursed me and the other doctors and finally left with her husband.

Epilogue
And The Story Continues

I was driving my son to school, for his post Covid offline classes. Schools were shut for almost two years. Though online classes were on, going to school, meeting friends and classmates, laughing, playing, teasing them, sharing notes and lunches with them, getting help from them to decide what subject to choose, what stream to opt for further higher studies were the most necessary everyday activities that they had missed in these two years.

I could relate to his feelings of loneliness without the company of his friends, and how he craved to speak to them and connect with them every day. We humans are social animals, and we need to be surrounded by the likes of us. Children love being with their peers, basking in the energetic and enthusiastic company of their friends. Interacting with your peers and hanging around with them is what contributes to one's mental development.

'Mom, I am beginning to realise that politicians are fools; politics is like an undirected play or circus going on all the time. I feel like they are trying to manipulate without even hiding the obvious wrongs. Do they think we are imbeciles? MPs jump like monkeys, from one party to another. It seems as if they have no morals. What is this reservation agenda that has delayed NEET counselling? Didi is disturbed because of so much uncertainty,' my son said to me on his way to school.

He had grown taller in these two years and more intelligent, too, I noted with pride. My daughter had appeared in a postgraduate entrance exam and had been waiting since eternity for counselling and seat allotment. The ever-present reservation conflicts in our education system are crippling it. The quota for castes, for low-income students, besides so many variables are also present that it has become frustrating for general category students.

Yes, politicians have now demanded some more reservations in medical schools. Already, we have more than 60 per cent seats reserved for a few specific castes, and now they are seeking to gift more seats to yet another category merely to increase their vote bank. We have numerous castes in our country, living together, interdependent on each other. But we are not united because these politicians have sown a seed of hatred and jealousy amongst us. They have made us realise that we belong to different castes. They have sown in us the thought that the general class thinks that they are superior by birth and that's why they are educated and earning well. So even if your child has obtained unimaginably low marks, he may have a secure a reserved seat because he belongs to a backward caste. And in the bargain, if a general category student scores many more marks and deserves that seat, he or she will be thrown out of the list, because there is actually no seat left in the general category. For example, if there are four seats, two are for SC, one for ST and one seat for OBC. This leaves absolutely no seat for general category students. How can that be justified?

Exactly thirty years ago, I too had suffered from this caste reservation that started with Mandal Ayog by V P Singh. Many protested, many were burnt alive or sacrificed their lives at a young age to condemn this ridiculous decision that eventually was turned into a law.

I wanted my kids to be doctors because it is a very gratifying profession. I tried to explain the merits of being a doctor to my daughter. But it seemed that history is repeating itself once again after thirty years. I can once again see the reservation drama being revived again. The flawed, unjust system, which shouldn't have been implemented in the first place, is still crippling the foundation of the education system, literally poisoning it. The most deserving, top scoring students are getting frustrated, while kids with quotas are securing good college seats without studying.

In this cat fight, only politicians are benefiting for the short-term. And for that term gain, they are compromising the country's future and digging the grave of our education system. There is continuous agitation, unrest and chaos among the younger population, and rage towards each other on the basis of caste. Politicians are using this situation to their advantage.

Yes, I too faced a similar fate while writing my PG entrance exam, exactly the same way as my daughter is suffering today. Counselling has been delayed after the exams because politicians are demanding some more reservation now, more than that already given. Protests erupted, and a case was filed

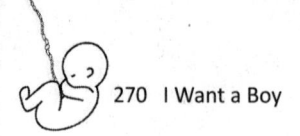

against them by GC students in the Supreme Court. Almost a year is about to pass, and no progress has yet happened. Medical colleges are struggling without new doctors and children are stuck at home even after securing good marks, as there is no certainty when the case will be settled, and whether the ruling will go in favour or against them.

Surprisingly, there has not been much media coverage of this important issue. Medical students are on strike, protesting this menace, even as patients are dying in government emergency OPDs due to scarcity of doctors. All this, while many aspiring young doctors are waiting to join hospitals. Yet, there is no news about any change in the offing. It seems even the media is on the payroll of politicians.

When political leaders of our country who are our law makers play foul, then the country is doomed. And that's why my daughter strongly insisted that my son should not prepare for his medical entrance. She finds it frustrating to see undeserving, low rankers, who were never studious students obtain seats in topmost medical schools like AIIMS.

'Mom, we don't have any seat left for us in AIIMS. Even if we score 100 per cent, there is not a single seat saved for GC in many subjects such as dermatology. Is it even justifiable in a court of law?' my children ask.

My daughter is now with a government hospital and there seems to be no change in them from the time I worked there—neither in the infrastructure, work environment or in the attitudes of government officials. From *aayas* to clerks to higher ranks, everyone seems to be functioning in the same style as they did thirty years ago.

My dog lover daughter on her first day on duty as a first-year resident OBGYN fed biscuits to stray dogs roaming in and around the hospital building. The next day, a trail of dogs was following her from bed to bed while she went on her rounds. She was a messiah for the dogs and they have been following her around the campus. So much so, that a patient even requested my daughter to shoo away a dog who had planted himself on a patient's bed, and was not allowing her to sit. My daughter was flabbergasted. Was that also a doctor's job in a government hospital?

In three months, she has lost eight kgs. All the running around is still part of the workload of the junior most residents. Clinical work exposure at the beginning is minimal, because these junior residents are the ones who deliver the blood samples to the lab, collect the reports, shift the patients, arrange blood, get forms signed, and follow nursing orders during their long hours of duty.

'Patients were overflowing in the OPDs. Labour rooms are always full. Mom, you need to follow the wailing of a patient or shouts from the nurses from which ever direction it is coming. The agony of a labouring mother is what pulled us to her bedside to conduct a delivery without wasting any time,' my daughter said, describing a typical day at a government hospital.

Acknowledgements

All these stories are real, though names have been changed to protect identities. I have highlighted the world inside a maternity ward in most government hospitals in India. The supply of medicines, suture materials, instruments, gloves and other medical accessories is meagre and inadequate and understandably, the residents there save all these items for emergencies. Laboratory tests are not conducted on an everyday basis and patients have to await their turn for surgeries, sometimes for reasons as frustrating as a non-functional ECG machine.

Our junior doctors don't have the luxury of wearing gloves, masks or using sterile surgical gowns due to frugal supply.

We residents work tirelessly, often without food, sleep and sometimes don't even have time to pee in our long, extended 36-48 hour shifts! An endless wave of patients floods every hospital, 24X7. Many of these patients are seriously ill after having been managed by quacks before they are brought in at the last stage to a big hospital. The spectrum of complications

in a pregnancy and during delivery are then manifested in several, severe forms.

Most of these are because of septic abortions or repeated child births. They were either avoidable or preventable.

The desire for a male offspring is no less among our rich, educated upper class who throng our costly corporate hospitals, as it is among our uneducated, or lower middleclass families.

I wanted to share these stories because this truth is often buried deep inside these hospitals, and it needs to be exposed and addressed more aggressively. Perceptions must change.

These stories are being enacted daily in real-life for the vast majority of our country's women—women who have no voice and are forced to succumb to the norm. My mother-in-law delivered three daughters in succession and was ill-treated by her in-laws, and was often oppressed even by her own family in front of her own sisters-in-law who delivered baby boys.

She was never treated well by her own joint family. So, I can quite well relate to her mental state upon seeing her granddaughter, even though, she was always loving towards her. However, she was carrying a past conditioning in her subconscious and this made her yearn for a grandson. But apart from this, she was relatively liberal with me and lovingly raised her granddaughter when I took off for further medical studies when she was born. In view of this, I believe I was lucky and couldn't have asked for better parents-in-law. They loved and respected me and my daughter and were always warm to my family.

And their son, my husband, remains a devoted partner in my journey and helped me blossom as a wife, a mother and a medical professional. Without him by my side, my education, my career and my practice would not have been possible. He has always supported me, and is the reason behind my success. He is a loving husband, a caring father and a thorough gentleman.

I am also lucky to have supportive and affectionate sisters and brothers-in-law. Their love has flowed in leaps and bounds for me, for my children, for my parents and sisters.

I am nothing without my mother. She is my rock–silent, strong, omnipresent, and omnipotent. She is my sounding board and is always comforting me with her wise, caring words and thoughts. On many occasions, she has stepped in to mother my children and has been the backbone of our family, holding it together. Personally, motherhood transformed me as a person, made me look beyond myself and helped me develop the qualities of patience and affection, helping me to give back to society and be a guide, and sometimes guarding the life of others. I am grateful to the universe for immersing and anchoring me in this powerful role. I thank God every day for bestowing upon me, the title of 'mother'.

My daughter, Irene, my first-born, was my first 'work' as a new mother. She is a better version of me, curated, cut and moulded to perfection. My son, my second-born who was raised more by his grandparents than by me, absorbed their better characteristics and took several traits from his *Didi* too. He has metamorphosed into a handsome boy with a profound and calm demeanour.

I am my father's girl, and that goes for all three of us sisters. He shielded us from the harsh world around us. We never knew or realised that being born as a daughter was any

different than being a son. We sisters, I, Pooja and Seema are the proud daughters of our father. His wisdom was echoed in his name, Ved. He passed on his philosophy of 'Impossible is nothing' to all three of us. 'Try with your heart, soul and mind,' he would tell us, and whatever we wanted would come searching for us!